Before Creation, Planet Life, After Life

DONZELLA ERVIN

ISBN 978-1-63844-542-5 (paperback)
ISBN 978-1-63844-543-2 (digital)

Copyright © 2021 by Donzella Ervin

All rights reserved. No part of this publication may be reproduced, distributed, or transmitted in any form or by any means, including photocopying, recording, or other electronic or mechanical methods without the prior written permission of the publisher. For permission requests, solicit the publisher via the address below.

Christian Faith Publishing, Inc.
832 Park Avenue
Meadville, PA 16335
www.christianfaithpublishing.com

Printed in the United States of America

But man dieth, and wasteth away: yea, man

Giveth up the ghost, and where is he?

Job 14:10

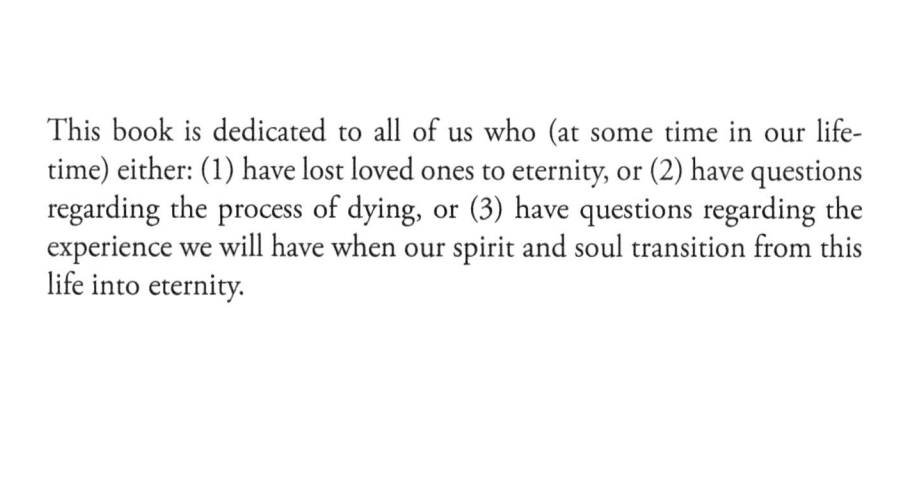

This book is dedicated to all of us who (at some time in our lifetime) either: (1) have lost loved ones to eternity, or (2) have questions regarding the process of dying, or (3) have questions regarding the experience we will have when our spirit and soul transition from this life into eternity.

Contents

Disclaimer		ix
Comments		xi
Foreword		xv
Preface		xvii
Chapter 1	Life's Cycles	1
Chapter 2	Fear Brings Torment	7
Chapter 3	Comfort One Another with These Words	11
Chapter 4	Eternal Life, Everlasting Life (In Him Is Our Life)	17
Chapter 5	The Resurrection	21
Chapter 6	I Will Prepare A Place for You	25
Chapter 7	Heaven	32
Chapter 8	The Place Called Hell	76
Chapter 9	The Necessity for Proper Warfare	81
Bibliography		87

Disclaimer

The writing of this book came about after the deaths of five of my family members during a ten-month period. And, as a result, I began searching for answers regarding life, death/dying, and eternity. And as you might expect, when someone is searching for something, they are usually doing it in uncharted territories for themselves, and many times, for others. This is the predicament I found myself in, when trying to harness my thoughts and bring them in line with God's word.

I wanted to know where we fit in eternity, both before we were born and after we leave this planet. The only way I could get a handle on the Scriptures and fit them into where *I thought* they may reference the above, was to create *a sort of lifecycle*, as it were.

I would like to admit that I probably have more zeal to know than Bible knowledge or scientific intellect. Most definitely, I do not purport to be a theologian, nor do I purport to be an authority on any of the topics chosen. I am simply a seeker of knowledge (as a Christian) as to where, I believe, my loved ones have transitioned and where I hope to go someday.

To accommodate this seeker approach (where I see that I am making statements or using Scriptures in a somewhat untraditional setting), I may present them as a question, leaving its relevance entirely up to you, the reader. I have done so, because I realize that we may disagree with my logic (as it relates to the Scriptures that I have selected to express a particular point). Apparently, my search does not offend God, because He invites me in Scripture saying, "If any of you is deficient in wisdom, let him ask of the living God (Who gives) to everyone *liberally* and *ungrudgingly*, without *reproaching*, or *faultfinding*, and it will be given him." (James 1:5, Amplified Bible [AMP])

I don't believe that God wants me to *pretend* that I don't have questions that concern me or threaten my peace of mind. In the books of Matthew 7:7 and Luke 11:9 He said, "AND I SAY UNTO YOU, Ask, and it shall be given you, seek, and ye shall find; knock, and it shall be opened unto you." This Scripture follows the parable about a friend (in his journey) needing bread and bread connotes the Word of God. Many of us have been on a long journey, and we are *in need of bread!* Even though many of our questions may only be answered when we see Him, but Jesus still invites us to "Come boldly before His throne (pursue Him) …." Matter-of-fact, I do mention in a few instances where I truly believe He spoke into my spirit a response that I never would have arrived upon with my own intellect.

So, let us *follow on to know Him* ….

"For our knowledge is *fragmentary* (incomplete and imperfect)" and "For now we are looking in a mirror that gives only a *dim (blurred) reflection* (of reality *as in a riddle* or enigma)". (I Corinthians 13:9 and 12, AMP)

Comments

I have known Pastor Donzella Ervin for over forty years and have had the utmost respect for her and her beloved husband, Richard. She is anointed and appointed of God in her own rights. This book is unique in that she is the author of it. When we think of a tenacious person as Pastor Ervin, we seem to forget that pastors are human too, and have human frailties just as others. We don't seem to think that someone who is as anointed as she is in deliverance would need prayer and deliverance also.

This book will be one of great deliverance for anyone who is in need of deliverance, after traveling the journey of losing a loved one, especially if they have been born-again. The spirit of comfort will be upon them after reading this book. The uniqueness of this journey is that she did not stop, but by the help of the Lord, wanted to walk it out. In walking it out, deliverance came to her and the same will come to others who will take the time to study and read this book.

In walking out this journey and authoring this book, Pastor Ervin has opened up the gateway for many answers to many questions that other Christians have had and have been afraid to ask.

Suffragan Bishop Joseph Cunningham
Greater Faith Temple
Benton Harbor, Michigan 49022

Before Creation, Planet Life, After Life is a practical book which can be used in both secular and Christian environments. As a therapist, serving both believers and non-believers in the area of counseling, I have had to walk the journey of grief when clients experience loss. Whether it is the loss of a loved one or a friend, I find that many have questions which may or may not be explainable. I had the privilege and honor of sitting under Pastor Donzella Ervin's teachings when she pastored Kingdom of God Tabernacle (KGT). It was during the time of her losses, whereby she had questions pertaining to death and dying, we all had many questions as well. Pastor Donzella (Pastor Emeritus-KGT) began to search the Scriptures and invited a guest speaker in to help us along this journey in experiencing loss. Pastor Donzella's book is a vital continuation to the teachings learned during her tenure. I highly recommend Before Creation, Planet Life, After Life, as a resource to anyone desiring to gain a better understanding of the death and dying process.

Bronwyn M Davis, MA. LPC &
Licensed EACM Minister

Donzella, thank you for touching my heart. Your book really has given me much to think about. It is interesting to see the different stories that the Lord gives us to strengthen our faith. I see a common theme that is the same; and the truth cannot be denied. All these stories, I believe, are intended to give us more faith to equip us to help others get to Heaven, like you say in your book. He gives us His Holy Spirit to guide us and lead us in this world, but I learned from your book, that there are forces out there seeking to devour us. Again, thank you. I have much to think about; but thank God for His word that says, "All things work together for the good of those who love the Lord."

Dr. Michael B.

As I read your manuscript, I found myself experiencing many "aha" moments that felt much like finding that illusive puzzle piece needed to complete the picture. I truly appreciate the offering of Scriptures looked at "outside the box" of traditional interpretation and looking into the dynamic reality of the Spirit with clarity and fresh revelation. Losing a loved one from a human standpoint seems so final and separating, but you have done a wonderful job disputing that illusion. Thank you for your faithful and thoughtful work, BEFORE CREATION, PLANET LIFE, and AFTER LIFE.

Pastor Jerry Moore
New Covenant Fellowship
Poplar Bluff, Missouri

What an AWESOME book! As one who has served under and been enriched through the teachings and writings of Pastor Donzella Ervin, I have to say that this book has been an eye opener for me concerning life after death! I now have a better understanding of what place to TRULY call my HOME!

I thank the Lord and count it an honor for Pastor Ervin to have chosen me as one of the people to have read such an astounding book before it hit the shelves, Internet, etc.! I thank God for her research and the revelation that He has given her and I pray that countless believers, as well as unbelievers, will be drawn closer to Jesus and receive a revelation of death and Heaven, as a result of reading this book.

Evangelist Kenyona Archibald
Farmington, Michigan

This book is very powerful and riveting! A "must read", by Pastor Donzella Ervin!

Dr. Keith L. Wagner

FOREWORD

I feel the need to, first, disclose my spiritual history in Christ, which began when I was baptized in the name of Jesus at the age of five and received the infilling of the Holy Spirit at age seven. The Holy Spirit also taught me to play the piano and by the age fifteen, the late Dr. Lottie Glenn, pastor of New Creation Church, asked me to become their musician. Initially, I could only play in one key and this often caused me to be embarrassed. So, in order to become a better musician, I asked Dr. Glenn if I could have a key for access to the church. I would come into the church and fall on my knees and pray for, however long the Holy Spirit was upon me, and then get upon the organ and place my hands on the keys, and the correct keys would immediately become illuminated before my eyes. Of course, I was simply amazed beyond human comprehension, while I watched what the Holy Spirit was revealing from the spirit realm.

Years passed, I became married, and the mother of three children; one son and two daughters. I later married Richard A. Ervin at the Greater Grace Temple of Detroit, Michigan, under the pastorate of the late Bishop David L. Ellis. After some years of service, we received the blessing of his son, Bishop Charles Haywood Ellis, III, to start our church (Kingdom of God Tabernacle) in Warren, Michigan.

We began to seek God for signs and miracles to be performed in that church, and God did some very unusual things before our eyes. However, there came a time of testing of our faith in another dimension that we had not anticipated, and that was death. During the time from September 25, 2014 to August 30, 2015 (ten months), I experienced five deaths in my immediate family; mother-in-law, son and grandson (car accident), youngest sister, and husband (Richard).

I gave my spiritual background to indicate that I should have had a normal reaction to death, if there is such a thing. Like so many pastors, I eulogized funerals of others, but when the death angel was allowed to attack my family so ferociously, it caused me to take introspection of their destiny. And, I might add that Job asked such a question of God saying, "But man dieth, and wasteth away: yea, man giveth up the ghost, and where is he?" (Job 14:10)

Preface

I think it would be beneficial for readers to know what initiated this writing. Our little church was already undergoing some big-time attacks from the enemy. (I believe it was because we were attempting to flow in the five-fold gifts of the Spirit). However, the final blow which practically shook my world apart was the sicknesses and deaths that took place so succinctly. Before I could focus on one incident, another was already upon the horizon.

On February 4, 2014, at 10:00 a.m., my youngest sister asked me to go with her and her husband as she went to Henry Ford Hospital in Detroit, Michigan, for an exploratory exam which she thought was an acid reflux condition. However, by 1:00 p.m., the exam revealed that she had pancreatic cancer in the fourth stage, and the doctor gave her only four months, at best, to live. She was told that neither radiation nor chemotherapy could help, because the cancer was so advanced.

I left my sister that day (at Henry Ford Hospital) and decided that I would stop by St. John's Hospital, where my husband was being treated for congestive heart failure. I thought I would visit him early on my way home, so I could attend Bible study that evening. When I walked into his room, which was by then 3:00 pm, the doctor called me back out into the hallway, telling me that I should "get my finances in order," because my husband had only a few more months to live. When I left my husband's hospital, I tried to drive home and my mind was so attacked that I drove right past my street. At that point, I began to plead with God for help to get home, because I could no longer think straight.

While we were in prayer and vigilance for the healing of my sister (who, according to the doctor's report, cancer was no longer in her body), my husband's mother passed away on September 25, 2014. My forty-four-year-old son came from his barbershop to view her body on October 4th, and by October 31st, he and his five-year-old son were killed on the way to a family timeshare vacation. Then, on January 15, 2015, my sister passed away from a stress-related condition (not the original cancer illness). Finally, on August 30, 2015, my husband, Richard, passed away.

In an earlier incident on August 26, 2008, my husband was hospitalized for heart surgery and died during the operation. However, the Holy Spirit reminded me of a prophetic word that had been given him previously, that "something was going to happen to him, but it would only be an illusion." So, we asked the doctor to "go back and open-up his chest again and do what he did best" and that "we would do what we did best." He agreed and called the surgical team back into the operating room, and in about one hour, after massaging his heart with his hand, Richard came back to life. The doctor tried to tell me that "we got him back upon the fence, but I don't think he will make it through the night." I told the doctor, "You didn't get him upon the fence, so you can't tell me if he's going to stay upon the fence." Needless-to-say, Richard had a full recovery from the surgery and God gave him seven years and four months longer to be on this planet.

When Richard's heart began to fail the last time, several ministers and our church members prayed prayers of healing for him, but I felt God wanted him home. And this is where I used the testimonies of the near death experiencers (NDEs or NDEers) that I read about, beginning when my son and grandson were killed. The first book I read was "Heaven is For Real" by Todd Burpo (and forty-one others at the time of writing this book). Some of them include numerous experiences of others by doctors or nurses, while many are solely writings of their own experiences (See Bibliography Page). I have prayed many prayers of thanks and blessings upon all those authors, who took the time to write their testimony, because their experiences gave me courage to release my husband into eternity, into the hands of an awesome God!

I think I should share one of my heart's dark secrets, which surfaced during this painful time. It is noteworthy, because it is one of the occurrences that caused me to pursue this search for understanding. After each of the funerals, my daughters stayed over to support me and help handle business. Of course, a part of that support happened to include our Sunday morning church service. At one service, I asked my oldest daughter to sing a solo, and she beautifully sang, "God is Able (and He Won't Fail)" by Smokie Norfolk. Ironically, the song made me angry and uncomfortable. I was relieved when it was over! The song made me realize the confusion of my heart and that I needed help; and I, surely, didn't want God to leave me in the emotional wilderness where I was. And in order for Him to mend my brokenness, I felt led to relinquish the pastoral leadership of the church, so that I could spend time with God and get healed.

After God took me by the hand and walked me through the Word (and leading me to read many of the experiences of the NDEers), I understood, more clearly, that His success is not limited by time and space, unlike ours. Often, we think He has failed because time has run out for it to: (1) come to pass in our time, (2) continue to exist on this planet, or (3) be seen with the natural eye. But "He Won't Fail," because He is able to bring His promises and desires to pass, being unhindered by time or space. Therefore, when we lose a loved one from this planet, God has not lost them at all! Their bodies may fade away and fail, but His faithfulness and love for that soul never fails! They have simply returned to the eternity from which they came. What God allowed me to experience has caused me to have an understanding of the many questions so many grieving souls were searching answers for (and many of them have yet to see a glimpse of light).

In Doctor Jeff O'Driscoll's book, "Not Yet (Near-Life Experiences & Lessons Learned)," he stated,

> "Most souls are searching for peace. Relatively few find it. To suggest a solution in brief anecdotes could only trivialize the problem and sound cliché. What impresses me—what changes me—is the realization that so many people are *in so much pain*. Pain, it seems, is the lowest common denominator in humanity. Pain, more than anything else, *makes us all alike*. What tears us apart is the naïve arrogance of thinking our own situation—*our own brand of pain*—is somehow different, *somehow more important than someone else's*.
>
> I sat with a tearful young man who admitted he just didn't know how to deal with the pain any longer. (The first anniversary of his brother's untimely death had just passed.) I knew little of the young man's life .... His whole countenance changed when he heard me say, 'I remember how I felt when *my brother died.*' As I spoke, hope returned to his face and confidence to his eyes." (Pgs. 102–104)

This pain, which seemed to be tailor-made for me, caused me to empathize as well as sympathize with the heartbroken. However, in my quest for answers, I found healing, wholeness, and compassion.

CHAPTER 1

LIFE'S CYCLES

THE CYCLES OF ETERNITY, LIFE, DEATH, AND ETERNITY
<u>(DEATH AND DYING SHOULD BE SEEN AS A PART OF LIFE)</u>

The purpose of this work should show the relevance of man's life's cycles as described in the Scriptures. However, in support of my theory, an article in an AARP publication, former astronaut, Jim Lovell, is quoted as saying, "It appeared to me that God had given mankind sort of a stage to perform on" (i.e. earth). My task in this first chapter will be to present Bible text to identify the various life cycles: (1) that eternity period that existed before man entered "our stage" (world), (2) *the time cycle* during our existence upon "our stage," (3) and how we exit "our stage" returning back into eternity.

Most of us would conclude that Genesis 1:1 and 2 are references enough to establish the existence of a pre-existing eternity from which God began to bring His word in (St. John 1:1–4) into what we would call "existence or time."

In the beginning God created the Heaven and the earth. (Genesis 1:1) (This also indicates that these two elements did not exist *before* God created them.)

And the earth was without form (had no definition), and void (empty, no life); and darkness was upon the face of the deep. (Genesis 1:2)

And the Lord God formed man out of the dust of the ground and breathed (either from His nostrils or mouth) into his (man's) nostrils the <u>breath of life (God's breath)</u>; and man became a living soul. (Genesis 2:7)

Paul seems to suggest that we existed somewhere on the side of eternity <u>*before*</u> the world was created, even if it was <u>*only in the mind of God.*</u> Notice the following verse which states:

> "According as he hath chosen us <u>*in him "before"*</u>
> the foundation of the world." (Ephesians 1:4)

I would like to suggest that this passage indicates that we were <u>*in His mind "before"*</u> the *foundation* of the world.

Paul confirms, further, that God was thinking about us and *making covenants* with us *"before"* the world was created and he was:

> "In hope of eternal life, (which God, that cannot
> lie), promised *"before"* the world began." (Titus
> 1:2)

God did not make this covenant or promise to the air or wind, but I would like to think that He saw us in His mind and made it to us. Therefore, we might have existed somewhere in eternity, even if it was only in the thought of God.

This Scripture could be much like where Jesus says to His disciples:

> "For the Father himself loveth you, because ye
> have loved me, and have believed that I <u>*came out
> from God. I came forth from the Father,*</u> and am

(now) come into the world: *(again)* I leave the
world, and go to the Father." (St. John 16:27–28)

Also, I would like to reference the story of Shadrach, Mechach, and Abednego in the book of Daniel:

"He (Nebuchadnezzar) answered and said, 'Lo, I see four men loose, walking in the midst of the fire, and they have no hurt; and the appearance of the fourth is like the Son of God.'" (Daniel 3:25, emphasis added)

Most evangelical Christians believe that this verse literally refers to the Son of God (Jesus Christ). Taking that position, then I would like to point out that the Father sent the Son *from* eternity *into* the world (in time) to deliver the three Hebrew boys who were experiencing the fiery furnace on planet earth. Afterward, Jesus *returned* to the Father in eternity to await the herald voice of the angel Gabriel to send Him *into the womb of the virgin Mary* (in time) on the planet. However, once His work of salvation was finished on calvary (in time), He *returned* to sit on the right hand of the Father (in eternity).

MY QUESTION IS THIS: Since Scripture says that Christ is our perfect example and Colossians 1:15 says that He was *"the first born of every creature"*, could this also mean that the process through which Jesus entered into time and returned back into eternity be that which we experience also?

LITTLE CHILDREN OFTEN ASK THE QUESTION: WHERE DO BABIES COME FROM?

ANSWER: And we gave such answers as "from (a stork) or mommy's tummy." But is this the true answer? Where did we come from **before** we entered our mother's womb?

Isaiah says, "For thus saith the high and lofty One that inhabiteth eternity ...." (Isaiah 57:15) And since He inhabits eternity, were we, at some point, in the thought of God (with Him and His thoughts) in eternity? **Before** we made our entry into this world, were we in the mind of God, even before we were manifested in the form of one of the million sperm cells (little heads and tails)?

King David said,

> "My <u>substance</u> was not hid from thee, when I was made in secret, and curiously wrought in the lowest parts of the earth.
>
> Thine eyes did see my <u>substance</u>, yet being <u>(unformed, un-perfect)</u>; and in thy book all my members were written, which in continuance were fashioned, when <u>as yet there was none of them </u>(only a thought in the mind of God).
>
> How precious also are thy thoughts unto **(of)** me, O'God! How great is the sum of them.
>
> <u>If I should count them, they are more in number than the </u>sand: when I awake **(am born or arrive in time)**, I am still with thee." (Psalm 139:15–18)

The prophet Jeremiah speaks of his pre-existence into the world, much like King David.

> "Then the word of the Lord came unto me saying, **Before** I formed thee in the belly, **I knew thee**;" (Jeremiah 1:4–5)

<u>**MY QUESTION IS THIS**</u>: Was He saying that Jeremiah was in His thoughts *before* he was conceived or *before* the foundation of the world was laid (similar to what Scripture says in Ephesians 1:3 and 4)?

Was our natural, as well as spiritual existence determined by God the Father and our Lord Jesus Christ **<u>in Heavenly places (eternity) IN Christ: … as he hath CHOSEN US IN HIM (BEFORE THE FOUNDATION OF THE WORLD (or eternity)?</u>** Was our spirits and souls in existence with the Father **before** the world was created, waiting to enter into time?

1 Corinthians 15:45 refers to Jesus being the second Adam and verse 47 indicates that He was not created by the hand of the Father out of the earth like the first Adam, rather He entered this world from (His eternity) into time through the womb of a human, and then when He exited this world, He went back into eternity. St. John 1:1 said, "The Word (Who was Jesus) was with God (the Father) in the beginning (<u>**eternity**</u> before there was a world creation), and the Word (Jesus) was God."

<u>**MY QUESTION IS THIS**</u>: Is the life cycle of Jesus Christ like that which we humans ("heirs to the Father and joint-heirs with the Son") **had *"before" the foundation of the world*, and are having in time, and some day will have in eternity**? The Scripture did say that Jesus "experienced everything in the flesh that we experienced." Could that experience encompass far more than what our human knowledge has been enlightened to imagine?

If you don't know your place of origin, how can you know where your destination will be? Job asks the question, **"But man dieth, and wasteth away: yea, man giveth up the ghost, and where is he?"** (Job 14:10) It is my opinion, that we came from eternity (the mind of God) and when we die, we will return to eternity (be it Heaven or hell).

Matthew responds to this question by stating: "And these shall go away into everlasting (eternal) punishment; but the righteous into eternal life." (Matthew 25:46) What so many people fail to acknowledge is that Jesus came that ALL MEN might have ETERNAL LIFE (IN ONE PLACE OR THE OTHER)! We might, hypothetically, say that Jesus is the life serum into every man's veins causing him to experience **eternity**. Regardless of whether you die a holy or wicked person, He is the reason for your eternal existence. Paul said, **"For as in Adam (because of Adam) ALL men die, so in Christ (because of Christ) ALL men shall be made alive."** (1 Corinthians 20:22) **Adam brought the curse of death to ALL men (whether they are** holy or wicked, i.e. ALL the inhabitants of this world); and Jesus did _conversely_ the opposite by bringing Eternal Life to ALL men whether they are holy or wicked (i.e. they will ALL experience Eternal Life, either in Heaven or hell).

Chapter 2

FEAR BRINGS TORMENT

(1 John 4:18 "… fear hath torment".)

That which is foreign to us, or that which we do not know or understand, causes us fear. And death has that effect upon most of us, whether we admit it or not; and/or whether we are experiencing the death of loved ones, or whether we are approaching death ourselves. Jesus informs us that we enter this world from somewhere else, just as he was from somewhere else, albeit two different places, "Ye are from beneath; and I am from above: ye are of this world; I am not of this world." (St. John 8:23) Basically, we could be considered "time travelers" when we enter this world.

However, of the forty-two books I have read on the subjects of Heaven, Death, and hell, (mostly written by near death experiencers (NDEs or NDEers) (See list on Bibliography Page), those NDEers affirm that they no longer have a fear of dying, as a result of their death experience. They tend to attribute this lack of fear to that which is no longer intimidating to them, but even more, to their visit to a place that they did not want to leave. Further, many have said that they can't wait for the day when they can return (home). We should note that often when our loved ones are in the process of transitioning from this earth, they refer to their journey as going home.

In Doctor Jeff O'Driscoll's book entitled, "Not Yet (Near-Life Experiences & Lessons Learned)," he tells of his friend Jeff's NDE and that "He went to a place of joy ...." *"It was familiar,"* he'd later write. *"It was home. .... There was <u>an ancient awareness</u>, as if I had <u>always been 'in this place</u>.'"* (*I Knew Their Hearts*, p. 31. of O'Driscoll's p. 90)

MY QUESTION IS THIS: Could this be what Jesus meant when He said, "And *where* I go you know, and *the way* you know." (St. John 14:4) Is it that our spirit knows *from where it came*, and, therefore, at the time of departure, it *"knows the way"* to take us *"home?"* Now, as you answer this question, also recall that, at the time of death, so many people say, *"I'm going home."* In my thinking, for someone to call a place (they wish to return to) "home," they would have had to inhabited or lived there, sometime prior. You can't (and don't) just arbitrarily call a place home, if in fact, it had never been your home before.

Also, while pondering the very process of dying (the human spirit and soul leaving the body), and struggling with how that could possibly feel, God spoke this question into my spirit, "Can you remember how it felt to take your first breath when you entered this world? Did it hurt? Did it burn? And I said, "No." Then, he said, "And you won't remember how it feels to take your last." As an aside, I would like to note here, how God can keep babies in water in the mother's womb, while not breathing any air for nine months and yet not allow them to drown. Can this mystery of life and death be one of the "manifold wisdoms (mysteries) of God," as spoken of in Ephesians 3:8–10?

When one woman was asked what her experience meant to her, she answered: "It changed my life. At a very early age I realized we are *two* people, physical and spiritual, and the spiritual body doesn't need the physical to survive. Knowing that has made me free." ("Dying to Wake Up," Dr. Rajiv Parti, p. 174)

Many of the NDEers had their experiences, as a result of a traumatic accident, but they all stated that they felt no pain as they exited the body. Only when their spirit and soul returned to the body did they feel pain. I would assume this occurs because pain is a human or an earthly phenomenon. I recall asking this question to one NDEer and received the response that "the spirit and soul are already gone," before the trauma can *terrorize* the body, as we would imagine. And, as many people like to say, that they were "with their loved one as they took their last breath," this NDEer explained that the loved one had been "gone before their last breath!" This response caused me to understand what the Apostle Paul was saying, (and we hear so often at funeral services), "O' death, where is thy sting (i.e. Greek—poison pain, trauma, affliction, fear, dread)? O' grave, where is thy victory?" (1 Corinthians 15:55) Jesus has intercepted the pain or terror that death had once afflicted upon us during the transition into eternity.

> "I will ransom them from the power of the grave; I will redeem them from death: O' death, I will be thy plagues; O' grave, I will be thy destruction: repentance shall be hid from mine eyes (i.e. I will have no change of heart or mercy)." (Hosea 13:14)

Paul wrote to Timothy stating that

> "…our Saviour Jesus Christ, who **hath abolished death (i.e. gotten rid of), and hath brought life and immortality to light (into existence)** through the gospel." (2 Timothy 1:10, KGV)

The Amplified Bible expresses the same basic thought, but when it gets to the word,

> "…our Saviour Jesus Christ," (it continues with) "Who ***annulled* death and made it of no effect and brought life and immortality (immunity from eternal death)** to light (into existence) through the gospel." (2 Timothy 1:10, AMP)

The Apostle Paul wrote to the church of the Thessalonians the following:

> "But I would not have you ignorant brethren, concerning them which are asleep (deceased), that ye sorrow not, even as others which have no hope.
>
> For if we believe that Christ died and rose again, even so them which sleep in Jesus will God bring with him.
>
> For the Lord himself shall descend **from Heaven** with a shout, with the voice of the archangel, and with the trump of God: and the dead in Christ shall rise first:
>
> Then we which are alive and remain shall be caught up together with them in the clouds, to meet the Lord in the air: **and, so shall we ever be with the Lord.**
>
> Wherefore, <u>comfort one another with these words</u>." (1 Thessalonians 4:13–18)

CHAPTER 3

COMFORT ONE ANOTHER WITH THESE WORDS

(1 THESSALONIANS 4:18)

We should begin this Chapter with Jesus Christ stating His purpose for coming to earth:

> "The Spirit of the Lord is upon me, because he hath *anointed me* to preach the *gospel* to the poor; *'he hath sent me to HEAL THE BROKENHEARTED ....'"* (Luke 4:18)

I don't believe that this order of purpose is coincidental, because the first correction we needed, after the fall of Adam and Eve, was to be given back that which was lost (put us in spiritual lack/poverty, made us poor). The second thing that man experienced, immediately after being driven out of the garden of Eden, was the murder and death of one of their sons, causing the first **BROKENHEARTEDNESS.** Is it because of the curse of Adam that God saw man's *brokenheartedness, beginning with Adam and Eve's loss of Abel?*

We have no idea as to how many people *have been* and *are* moving around in this earth in a brokenhearted state of mind (in one form or another). When speaking of death, divorce, and most any kind of family separation, the first reaction we experience is *to ask why* because we know that *God could have stopped it*, then follows *anger* for pretty much the same reason. Next come *our failed attempts at creating "the new normal"* without our loved ones in the picture. And finally, we move into *a life of loneliness*, once we resolve that there is nothing we can do to change what has taken place.

The prophet Isaiah gives very comforting words to those of us who lose loved ones,

> "The righteous man perishes, and no one lays it to heart; and the merciful and devout men are taken *from the* calamity and evil to come (even sometimes through wickedness).
>
> **He (in death) enters into peace;** *they rest in their beds,* **each one who, walks straight and in his uprightness."** (Isaiah 57:1–2, AMP)

Apostle John spoke these words of comfort to the church, as it pertains to their death:

> "And I heard further (perceiving the distinct words of) a voice from **HEAVEN**, saying, **'Write this: Blessed (happy, to be envied)** *are the DEAD* **(from now on)** *who die in the Lord!* **Yes, blessed (happy, to be envied indeed),** *says the Spirit,* **(in) that they may rest from their labors, for their works (deeds) do follow (attend, accompany) them!'"** (Revelation 14:13, AMP)

Jesus promises that "He that liveth and believeth in me *shall NEVER DIE."* (St. John 11:26) These are the Lord's words of promise to his people. What we must know is that when man fell in the Garden of Eden, Adam and Eve's body and soul remained alive, but their spirits died *"the very day that they disobeyed."* God spoke to me and said, "If I could keep the body and soul alive, **while their spirits were dead,** why can't I let the body die **and keep the soul and spirit alive?"** We trust doctors who did not give us life to put us asleep, believing they will wake up again to this life. But the God, who gave us life, we do not believe.

Jesus speaks about the eternal life and protection that He promises to *His* sheep:

> "And I *give unto them "eternal life"; and they shall NEVER PERISH, neither shall any man "PLUCK" (take) them out of my hand.*
>
> My Father, which gave them (to) me, **is GREATER THAN ALL; and NO MAN IS ABLE TO "PLUCK" THEM OUT OF "MY FATHER'S" HAND.**
>
> I and my Father are one." (St. John 10:27–30)

Neither can death "pluck" us out of His hand from the time we enter into the mind of God, before we enter into time, and after we exit this planet.

"Precious in the sight of the Lord is the death of *His* saints." (Psalm 116:15) This would lead me to believe that *He pays "special attention to this transition and that He watches over it."* And David goes on to say that: "he preserveth the souls of *his* saints." (Psalm 97:10) (i.e. keeps them throughout eternity). They are not allowed to be tormented nor destroyed by death. David speaks, further, of "the Lord being our Shepherd" (Psalm 23) and us not having to want (be in need) for anything, even for life itself! The Good Shepherd moves sheep from one place to another *(even through time into eternity)*, and He provides for their needs all along the way.

Even when we have to *walk through the "valley of the shadow of death,"* the only thing we deal with is the shadow, because "our Saviour Jesus Christ, **hath ABOLISHED (gotten rid of) death,** and

hath BROUGHT LIFE, and IMMORTALITY to light (existence) through the gospel." (2 Timothy 1:10)

As we learn more about His word concerning death, *and that death is "only a mirage,"* we can conquer the fear of, loneliness from, and physical trauma it once held over us. The dictionary defines **"a shadow" as a temporary place to the real.** [To literally do the **walk through** the valley, you have to **enter it "at or from some point,"** then move forward and proceed toward the **outer point into that which is no longer considered "the valley!"**]

MY QUESTION IS THIS: Is the "valley of the shadow of death" spoken of in the Psalm 23:4, Isaiah 9:2, and Matthew 4:16, that "dark tunnel or window" that some NDEers say they traveled through prior to entering an "inexplicable bright light?"

I seem to recall from some biology text book that there was a poisonous field or space of air surrounding the earth's surface (i.e. between earth and the outer space). As I pondered this concept, I thought that I heard in my spirit, "Go to the first chapter of Genesis and see if this poisonous air or darkness was mentioned after God finished creating the world." If you read those first few verses, it doesn't say anything about a poisonous layer of air or darkness being left in place, after God finished creating the world. Before Adam and Eve sinned, every reference God made to His creation was that it "was good and very good."

On April 10, 2019, I happened to be watching Fox 2 News as the newscaster was airing a clip made by a group of scientists who believe they proved Einstein's theory of the existence of a **Supermassive Black Hole in the Universe**, with **an actual visual image of that hole (Astro Physical Letter in the Boston Herald, dated April 10, 2019 and updated April 11, 2019).** These scientists unveiled the **first ever IMAGE OF A BLACK HOLE—featuring a ring of light bending as it is DRAWN INTO A CIRCLE OF DARKNESS— and a scientist involved with the collection said this helps create a road map to seeing what's in the middle of our galaxy, the Milky Way.**

So, I googled information on the **Supermassive Black Hole** where questions were being asked like these:

1. **What creates a Supermassive Black Hole?**

"The majority of the mass growth of **Supermassive Black holes** is thought to occur through episodes of rapid **gas accretion (disk)**, which are observable as **active galactic nuclei** or **quasars** .... THIS SUGGESTS THAT SUPERMASSIVE BLACK HOLES *AROSE (MATERIALIZED, DEVELOPED), VERY EARLY IN THE UNIVERSE*, **inside the FIRST MASSIVE GALAXIES.**"

2. **How many Black Holes are there?**

"There are so many black holes in the Universe that it is impossible to count them. It's like asking how many grains of sand are on the beach."

3. **How massive are these Black Holes?**

"**Supermassive Black Holes** are a million to a billion times **more massive than our Sun** and are found in the center of galaxies."

In Dr. Rajiv Parti's book, "Dying to Wake Up," he said: "I passed through a field of white light .... Then the light faded, and I went into **a deep darkness, one so dark it was palpable. To me it felt like a 'black hole', a void of emptiness and nothingness.**" (p. 214)

<u>**HERE, AGAIN, IS MY QUESTION:**</u> Could it be that, after the fall of Adam and Eve, darkness came upon the earth as that layer of atmosphere, and was formed around the earth in response to God's curse upon the earth? Did it come into existence for the sole purpose of causing death to hover over the planet, and everything in the earth would eventually die, as a result of this curse? Also, is this the "valley of the shadow of death" (or death zone) that every

human must pass through in route to the heavens? Remember Scripture says:

> "But there went up a mist from the earth and watered the whole face of the ground." (Genesis 2:6)
>
> "And out of the ground made the Lord God to grow every tree that is pleasant to the sight, and good for food ...." (Genesis 2:9)

However, notice the **words spoken by God after Adam sinned**,

> "Cursed is the ground *'for thy sake'*" (Genesis 2:17) and "Thorns and thistles shall it bring forth *to thee* ...." (Genesis 2:18)

Because of Adam, **death** and **darkness** covered the whole planet (as well as all animals and vegetation). But "The people **WHICH SAT IN DARKNESS** *SAW GREAT LIGHT;* **AND TO THEM WHICH** *SAT IN THE REGION AND 'SHADOW OF DEATH'* **LIGHT IS SPRUNG UP."** (Matthew 4:16) Furthermore, John said, "In him (Jesus) **WAS LIFE;** and *'THE LIFE'* **WAS THE 'LIGHT OF MEN."** (St. John 1:4) The word states, "For as in Adam **ALL DIE (ALL *LIVING THINGS);* EVEN SO** in Christ **SHALL (*ALL LIVING THINGS)* BE MADE ALIVE."** (1 Corinthians 15:22)

CHAPTER 4

ETERNAL LIFE, EVERLASTING LIFE (IN HIM IS OUR LIFE)

The word of God comforts us saying that, Jesus Christ *is our earnest down payment* on eternal life:

> "He who believes in the Son of God (who adheres to, trusts in, and relies on Him) has the testimony **(possesses this divine attestation)** within himself. He who does not believe God (in this way) has made Him out to be *and* represented Him as a liar, because he has not believed (put his faith in, adhered to, and relied on) the evidence **(the testimony)** that God has borne regarding His Son.
>
> And this is that testimony **(that evidence): God gave us eternal life, <u>and this life is in His Son.</u>**
>
> He who possesses the Son has that life; he who does not possess the Son of God **does not have that life.**
>
> I write this to you who believe in (adhere to, trust in, and rely on) the name of the Son of God (in peculiar services and blessings conferred by Him on men), <u>**so that you may know (with settled**</u>

> <u>**and absolute knowledge) that you (already) have life, yes, eternal life."**</u> (1 John 5:10–13)
>
> "And we (have seen and) know (positively) that the son of God has (actually) come to this world and has given us understanding *and* insight (progressively) to perceive (recognize) *and* come to know better and more clearly Him who is true; and we are in Him Who is true—in His Son Jesus Christ (the Messiah). This (Man) is the true God and life eternal." (1 John 5:20, AMP)

As we live on this planet, we need to assuredly know the word of God concerning His promises to us for our transition into eternity. The saints, of years ago, used to sing a little song that goes like this:

> You've got to live forever, somewhere; You've got to live forever, somewhere;
>
> With the angels in Heaven or with the demons in hell; But you've got to live forever somewhere.

1 Corinthians 15 could read almost "like" **Jesus Christ is a spiritual life serum to humanity.**

> **"For as in Adam ALL die, even so in Christ ALL (live) shall be made alive."** (1 Corinthians 15:22)
>
> **"The first man Adam was made a living soul; the last Adam was made a quickening spirit."** (1 Corinthians 15:45)

Jesus Christ <u>BRINGS ETERNAL LIFE TO "EVERYMAN,"</u> whether it be to eternal life or eternal damnation.

> "He (Jesus Christ) is not the God of the dead, but of the living, **for to him <u>ALL ARE ALIVE</u>.**" (Luke 20:38)

Jesus confirms that eternal life is predicated upon one's faith in the Father and Son.

> "He that heareth my word, and believeth on him that sent me, **hath <u>everlasting life (eternal life—no beginning and no end</u>)** and shall not come into condemnation; but is passed from death unto life.
>
> When the dead (sleep) shall hear the voice of the Son of God: and they that hear shall live.
>
> **For as the Father (creator) hath life in himself, <u>so hath he given to the Son to have life in himself.</u>**" (St. John 5:24–26)

During my early years of ministry, I had the occasion to preach the eulogies of my mother (eighty-one years old) and my father (ninety-four years old). However, these deaths occurred ten years apart, thus, allowing me some time to grieve and adjust to the loss. Also, I had the surviving parent to cling to, during the process. The entirely different situation, of the pain and misunderstanding from losing five family members in the short space of ten months did not allow me space to catch my breath. But it did prompt me to ask the question like Job, **"But man dieth, and wasteth away: yea, man giveth up the ghost, AND WHERE IS HE?"** and, in so doing, to research this topic.

The Apostle Paul says: "For I am persuaded, that neither death, nor life, nor … shall be able to separate us from the love of God …." (Romans 8:38) Many of us Christians are braced for death, as it pertains to this verse (for ourselves), however, when it attacks our loved ones, often the pain of death or lack of understanding of God's word concerning death can cause a gulf or breach between ourselves and God. As I mentioned earlier, we first ask God why; then we become angry (that He allowed it to happen, knowing full well that He could have stopped it); and then we flat out blame Him for it!

I asked God *not to* let some minister lay hands on me to cast out the spirits of grief and pain, but that He would take me by the hand and **"walk me through 'the valley of the shadow of death.'"** I wanted to understand the process of life, time, and death (i.e. the life cycle), or just plainly spoken, **"When my loved ones transitioned to be with the Father and Jesus, what did they experience?"** And, God favored me by making available to me the writings of so many NDEs; and lastly, literally placing one NDEer in my life to explain away many of my questions in exchange for peace and an enlightened mind.

Chapter 5

THE RESURRECTION

Jesus continues speaking about the resurrection of the dead and the wicked.

> "And shall come forth; they that have done good, <u>**unto the resurrection of life**</u>; and they that have done evil, <u>**unto the resurrection of damnation.**</u>" (St. John 5:27–29)

Paul writes to that church the following comforting words:

> "But I would not have you to be ignorant brethren, concerning them which are asleep, **that you sorrow not, even as others which have no hope. Christ died and rose again (He being the first fruit of the dead), even so them also <u>which sleep in Jesus</u>** will God bring with him.
>
> For the Lord himself shall descend **from Heaven** with a shout, with the voice of the archangel, and with the trump of God: and **the dead in Christ shall rise first:**
>
> Then we which are alive and remain shall be caught up **together with them in the clouds, to**

> **meet the Lord in the air: and so shall we ever be with the Lord.**
>
> Wherefore, comfort one another with these words." (1 Thessalonians 4:13–18)

In St. John 11:1–44 the story is told of Lazarus, Martha and Mary. Specifically, in verses 21 and 22 Martha comments on Jesus's delay in coming to heal her brother and that if He had come earlier, he would not have died. And in verse 22 she continues by telling Jesus, "But I know that even now, whatsoever thou wilt ask of God, God will give it thee."

> Jesus saith unto her, "Thy brother shall rise again."
>
> Martha saith unto him, "I know that he shall rise again in the resurrection at the last day."
>
> Jesus saith unto her, ***"I am the resurrection, and the life: he that believes in me, though he were dead, yet shall he live:***
>
> ***And whosoever liveth and believeth in me shall never die. Believest thou this?"*** (St. John 11:23–26)

THIS IS WHERE ONE OF MY QUESTIONS EMERGED: We have heard this text preached at many, if not most, home-goings; but after my up-close-and-personal experience with those five deaths, I began to ponder about its true meaning to us as God's creation. And I rolled it over and over in my mind, continually asking God what it meant as it related to **"believing on him and never dying**?" He took me to the book of Genesis where it reads:

> "And the Lord commanded the man, saying, 'You may freely eat of every tree of the garden;

> But of the tree of the knowledge of good and evil, thou shalt not eat of it: ***for in the day that thou eatest thereof thou shalt surely die.***" (Genesis 2:16–17)

I continued to think about and compare these two Scriptures wherein one says: **"Whosoever liveth and believeth in him shall never die,"** yet we who believe, continue to die physically. And on the other hand, God said that **"In the (very day) that thou eatest thereof thou 'shalt surely die.'"** But Adam and Eve's *physical bodies* continued to live, procreate, build, etc. Not until many years later, did they die physically.

The Holy Spirit began to enlighten these two verses to me by explaining the mystery of the three parts of man. He explained that *the spirit* of man died **in the (very day)** Adam and Eve disobeyed God.

> "For as **in Adam "ALL DIE," even so in Christ 'SHALL ALL BE MADE ALIVE.'"** (1 Corinthians 15:22)

(A side bar thought here: Recall that Jesus's name in Matthew 1:23 was Emmanuel, **meaning "GOD WITH US."** Once we receive Jesus Christ as our Saviour and Lord, He causes our spirit man to *become **ALIVE*** by making His abode in us.)

The Holy Spirit, also brought to my attention Ephesians 2:1, wherein Paul was speaking to people who were *physically alive*, and hearing him teach in the synagogues, but they *(were spiritually DEAD, even as Paul was speaking to them)* had shared in the death of Adam.

> "And you hath he quickened (resurrected), **who were dead (in trespasses and sins)."** (Ephesians 2:1)

These two Scriptures helped me visualize **the mystery of how we can die in the physical and yet REMAIN "ALIVE" IN THE SPIRIT AND SOUL *AND NEVER DIE!***

The Apostle Peter gives a further example that we can be separated from the physical man and yet **the spirit and soul remain "ALIVE."** Jesus's body was dead in a tomb in Rome, *BUT HIS SPIRIT AND SOUL "WENT DOWN" INTO PRISON (SHEOL).*

> "For Christ also hath once suffered (crucified) for sins, the just for the unjust, that he might bring us to God (restored life eternal); **being put to DEATH IN THE FLESH, (but) QUICKENED by the SPIRIT:**
>
> **BY WHICH (ALSO) HE *WENT AND PREACHED UNTO THE SPIRITS (dead people) IN PRISON (HELL).*"** (1 Peter 3:18–19)

CHAPTER 6

I WILL PREPARE A PLACE FOR YOU

The Heaven or paradise God prepared for us was the Garden of Eden. However, sin aborted this plan. Genesis tells the fate of the human race;

> "So he drove out man; and he placed at the east of the Garden of Eden Cherubims, and a flaming sword which turned every way (direction), **to keep the way of the tree of life**." (Genesis 3:24)

But Jesus restores to us entry back into the Garden of Eden (or Heaven/paradise),

> "To him that overcometh **will I _give to eat (allow) of the tree of Life, which is in the midst of the paradise of God_**." (Revelation 1:7)

At the outset, I admit I questioned whether Heaven and paradise are one and the same. When the thief was dying next to Jesus, Jesus promised him,

> **"Today shalt thou be with me in _paradise_."** (Luke 23:43)

In 2 Corinthians 12:1–4, it tells of Paul's NDE such that in verse 2, he refers to **being caught up to the "THIRD HEAVEN."** Then he continues to tell of his experience in verses 3 and 4, and describes the place as **how that he was caught up "into paradise."**

There is no reference to the place called **"paradise"** in the Old Testament. The only three references to it are found in the New Testament. The Greek word for this place is **paradeisos (par-ad-i-sos); of Oriental or a park; an Eden (place of future happiness).**

In Genesis 5:24 the Scripture speaks about God taking Enoch **UP**, but does not specifically name the destination as being **Heaven**, though we as Christians regard that as an "accepted fact." However, the Scripture clearly refers to **Heaven** as Elijah's destination, "and Elijah went **UP** by a whirlwind '**into HEAVEN.**'" (2 Kings 2:11)

Jesus said, "Let not your heart be troubled: ye believe in God, believe also in me." (St. John 14:13) Jesus was dispelling the fears that we face when exiting this world and are transitioning to the next. Because, before Jesus went away to prepare this place for us, **there was no place for us after:**

1. The fall of Adam which separated us from God; and
2. According to Genesis 3:24, we were **driven out of our place**—lost access to **the place God created (designed or prepared) for us.**

In the second verse, in my Father's house (place of existence) (which is outside of the existence of all the worlds He has made) **ARE MANY MANSIONS (worlds—galaxies—stratosphere—cosmos) that, at the time, does or does not exist.**

In the book, The Boy Who Came Back From Heaven, by Kevin and Alex Malarkey, Alex informed us in his story about the following:

> "For instance, Heaven is not the *"next"* world; it is *now*. Heaven is not in *"the heavens"* or the sky.

BEFORE CREATION, PLANET LIFE, AFTER LIFE

> It is ***everywhere*** and ***nowhere.*** Alex says it's hard to explain.
>
> Our earthly minds struggle to understand a *"place"* that is *"not a place"* and a *"time"* with *"no past, present, or future, but only **ETERNAL NOW. THE EARTH, THE SKY, THE COSMOS, AND TIME"***—these are things that God made. They are the home He made for us, and He enters into them to interact with us, ***BUT HE DOESN'T LIVE IN SPACE OR TIME.***" (p.176)

Halley's Bible Handbook, Chapter on Genesis, **"BEGINNING OF THE WORLD, MAN ...."** (p. 59).

> "**EVERY CHILD ASKS THIS QUESTION: AND NO ONE CAN ANSWER IT. THERE ARE SOME THINGS BEYOND US.** We cannot conceive of the Beginning of Time nor the End of Time, nor the Boundaries of Space. The world has been in existence Always, or, it was Made out of Nothing; one or the other, yet we can conceive Neither." (p. 59)

Under the topic which Halley discusses **The Universe Which God Created**, he states the following:

> "Astronomers estimate that **the Milky Way, the Galaxy** to which our earth and solar system belong, contains over **30,000,000,000 suns**, (many of them immensely larger than our sun, which is a million and a half times larger than earth. **The Milky Way** is shaped like a thin watch, its diameter from rim-to-rim being **200,000 light years:** (a light year is the distance that travels in a year at the rate of **186,000** miles per second). *AND*

THERE ARE, AT LEAST, 100,000 GALAXIES LIKE THE MILKY WAY, SOME OF THEM (LIGHT-YEARS APART). AND ALL THIS MAY BE (ONLY) (A TINY SPECK) (IN WHAT IS BEYOND) (IN THE (INFINITE), (ENDLESS) STRETCH OF SPACE!" (p. 60)

According to Genesis 1:6–8, as explained in Halley's Bible Handbook, "The Firmament called **'HEAVEN,'** here, *means the Atmosphere, OR LAYER OF AIR, between the water-covered earth and the clouds above, made possible by the cooling of the earth's waters, still warm enough to make clouds that hid the Sun.*"

Genesis 1:1 says, "In the beginning God created **the Heaven** and the earth." However, Genesis 2:1 says, "Thus **THE HEAVEN(S)** and the earth were finished, **and (ALL the host of them).**" There is no term for Heaven in Greek, but there are two in Hebrew. The first is **shamayim;** dual of an unused singular. The second is **shameh (shawmeh);** from an unused root meaning **to be** *lofty;* **the sky** (*as a loft*)**; the dual sphere. Alluding to the visible arch in which the clouds move, as well as to the higher ether where the celestial bodies revolve): air, [x] astrologer, heaven(S).**

In Hebrews, Apostle Paul speaks of **WORLD(S).**

> "Hath in these last days spoken unto us by His Son, whom he hath appointed heir of all things, by whom also he made **the WORLD(S)**." (Hebrews 1:2)

He continues:

> "Through faith **we understand (realize and believe) that the WORLD(S) WERE framed (created, fashioned)** by the word of God ...." (Hebrews 11:3)

King Solomon states,

> "But will God in very deed (truly) dwell with men on earth? behold, **Heaven and the HEAVEN OF HEAVEN(S)** cannot contain thee ...." (2 Chronicles 6:18)

Apostle Peter speaks about **the HEAVEN(S),** *OUT OF THE WATER and IN THE WATER:*

> "But the day of the Lord will come as a thief in the night; in which **the HEAVEN(S)** shall pass away with a great noise, and the elements shall melt with a fervent heat ....
>
> Looking for and hasting unto the coming of the day of God, wherein **the HEAVEN(S)** being on fire shall be dissolved, and the elements shall melt with fervent heat?
>
> Nevertheless we, according to his promise, look for **new HEAVEN(S)** and new earth, wherein dwelleth righteousness." (2 Peter 3:5)

Apostle John, the Revelator, tells us of a **HEAVEN** that he either saw in a vision or God took him **UP.**

> "And I saw **a NEW HEAVEN** and a new earth for THE **FIRST HEAVEN** and the first earth were passed away.
>
> And I, John, saw the holy city, **NEW JERUSALEM, coming DOWN from GOD OUT OF HEAVEN, prepared (created, fashioned) as a bride adorned for her husband.**" (Revelation 21:1–2)

Apostle Paul states that Jesus,

> "...having made peace through the blood of his cross, by him to **reconcile all things unto himself; by him, I say, whether they be things in earth, or things in Heaven.**
>
> **And you, that were sometime alienated and enemies in your mind by wicked works, yet now hath he reconciled.**
>
> **In the body of his flesh through death, to present you holy and unblameable and unreproveable in his sight (now worthy to occupy <u>"a place"</u> in his '<u>Father's house</u>)."** (Colossians 1:20–22)

So, Jesus came on the scene to reconcile us back to God the Father. **And now that we are His, He has the responsibility of a father (husbandman) to provide <u>"a place"</u> for His children (and/or bride).**

Apostle Paul says:

> "Therefore, if any man be in Christ, **he is a new creature:**
>
> And all things **are of God, who hath reconciled us to himself by Christ Jesus,....**" (2 Corinthians 5:17–20)

Now we are <u>ambassadors for Christ</u> (i.e., new citizenship from His world, so we must have <u>"a place"</u> to return to after our assignments are finished). <u>Before</u> Christ, those in the faith died being strangers and pilgrims on earth.

Apostle Paul says that,

> "These all died in faith, not having received the promises, but having seen them afar off, **and were persuaded of them (confident in them), and**

> embraced them, and <u>that they were strangers and pilgrims "on the earth."</u>
>
> For they that say such things declare plainly **<u>that they seek "a country."</u>**
>
> **<u>But now they desire "a better country," that is "HEAVENLY":</u> wherefore God is not ashamed to be called their God: <u>for he hath prepared for them A CITY.</u>**" (Hebrews 11:13–16)

In times past, God's people looked for, longed for, and anticipated their move to Heaven! Today, however, there is no **<u>inward</u>** or **<u>outward</u>** desire or plan to go there! Many of the testimonies from the saints during church services would include some desire to "see the face of Jesus who loved and died for them" or "to see the place that He went away to prepare for them." Today, we want a better paying job, a bigger house, more up-to-date vehicle, or to become one of the "rich and famous," etc.

Chapter 7

HEAVEN

(KINGDOM OF GOD TABERNACLE'S QUESTION AND ANSWER SESSION WITH DEAN BRAXTON)

Dean and his wife, Marilyn, introduced themselves to us by showing a video which was made for them by the 700 club. This video showed how Dean's spirit left his body during a procedure he was having done in the hospital, and as a result, he was clinically diagnosed as dead by the physicians.

> Me and my wife, Marilyn, had the privilege of being on the 700 Club. They came out and did a story on us. Now, you've got to understand, they did not just come out and do a story about a man who died and went to Heaven. For six months, they investigated us. They looked at the medical records. They talked to the people. They wanted to make sure that what we were saying for the first five years were true. And people ask, "What do you mean for the first five years?" For the first five years, we did not get a doctor to come forward and say this is what happened to us. The

reason is because when I went in the hospital, they made the mistakes. They were afraid that we were getting information so that, later on, we could come back and do litigation. And no medical person wanted to touch us for a long time. But I figured that after five years, they thought, "He has not come by now; he's not coming."

See, I always tell people, "You go to Heaven, and see who you sue!" This place is falling apart! If you've got the greatest house in the world, it's still going to need maintenance, and I was in a place where nothing needed maintenance! There is no deterioration in heaven. So, my mindset was not to get the information to sue them. When Marilyn and I went to them to get the medical records, they thought we were getting the records so we could have a court case. But we were getting the records, so we could tell people how good our God is!

A lot of people like to say, "You've got a great testimony." First of all, it's not my testimony; it's His! I just laid there! He did the work! My wife did pray, but He did the work! Most of us don't realize it's not our testimony; it's His! We just get the privilege of telling how great our God is through the testimony of our lives. A lot of times, we take ownership of it. No. It's His. The reason I'm saying this is because a lot of us have testimonies and we put them on the shelf. We think because they happened a long time ago, and you told a lot of people, you ought not to tell them anymore. No. There are no old testimonies.

Last night the pastor was telling us some things that happened a long time ago, and we were just as excited then, as though it just happened a few years ago!

QUESTION: WHEN DID YOU HAVE YOUR EXPERIENCE?

DEAN'S ANSWER:

I had it almost ten years ago, May 5, 2006. Some people ask me, "Aren't you forgetting some of the things you (saw, heard, smelled, felt) experienced?" No. As I get closer to home, I'm remembering more. It's like anybody who goes away for a while, but as they get closer to home, they become excited and things come back to their remembrance that they thought they'd even forgotten.

QUESTION: AND YOU HAVE NO FEAR OF RETURNING HOME?

DEAN'S ANSWER:

No.

QUESTION: EXPLAIN TO US THE DIFFERENCE BETWEEN AN "*OUT-OF-BODY*" EXPERIENCE AND A PERMANENT "*SEPARATION*" OF SPIRIT AND SOUL FROM THE BODY.

DEAN'S ANSWER:

An out-of-body experience (NDE) is different from a separation. When there is a separation, it is when the body dies and you leave it, until the resurrection day. However, a NDE is when the spirit and soul is allowed to return to the body, while remaining on this planet.

So, I can prove that I died, but where I went is the important thing. But because I knew Jesus Christ, as my Lord and Saviour, and His Spirit resides down on the inside of me, I went where real Christians are supposed to go. I went to Heaven where Jesus is. It is not unusual for Christians to go to Heaven. That's where were supposed to go, when our spirit leaves our bodies. And if my wife had not done all that she was supposed to do, I was "not in a bad place!" To be honest with you, I was "more alive there" than here. I didn't have to fool around with this flesh any longer. Because, whether you realize it or not, your flesh is "not going to Heaven." Again, I did not go to a "bad place" and "I did not want to come back!" And it wasn't because I didn't love my wife and children. I love them more than you can imagine. It's because, "there, everything is right! There's nothing wrong!" It's past peace! "There's nothing to be peaceful from!" Philippians 4:7 says that we can have "peace, which passeth all understanding," and I was in a place where "there is nothing to be peaceful from," and I fit in.

Dean said he wasn't afraid to die, and he told himself when it happened, "I am dying," when he first entered Heaven (because he went to Heaven several times). He said, "I will tell you the truth, I was planning on staying in Heaven, but the doctor kept on working on me, and said he didn't know why."

His wife prayed, and *she directed* the people as to "how they were to pray" for him. Dean said, "She had to 'battle' for me. She had to set-up a war strategy, not for only me being back on the planet, but that I was perfectly healed. I have no illnesses. For the next three days, after hearing what she refused to receive as true from the doctors, she battled in prayer for his life, "hard, long and loud!" Also, Marilyn did not allow anyone in Dean's room without her permission. She had to know that you were agreeing with the prayers and faith that she had for Dean's life. As a result of these prayers, Dean is not only back on the planet, but God has healed him of all the twenty-nine things that were supposed to be wrong with him after this situation.

During my hospitalization, the doctors came to my wife many times saying, "This is going to happen and that's going to happen." She would in turn, respond to them, "It doesn't have to be that way." The doctors were doing what they could do, and she could have conceded to their diagnosis. But she insisted that, "It didn't have to be that way." She wasn't thinking from an earthly point of view. She was thinking from an Heavenly point of view. And guess what happened? She obtained Heavenly results!

Dean said that he does not lay claim to God's miracle of his return to this planet as "his testimony." But he said it was because his wife and other people she called were praying. He said, "Some people want to believe that we, as people of God, have no say in what goes on in the spirit world, but that's not true." The Scripture says, "Thy will be done in earth (by prayer) as it is in Heaven." We have a part to play. You are the person to make it manifested in this realm.

DEAN BEGINS HIS TEACHING:

> One of the first Scriptures I am going to use is found in St. John 14:1–2 (KGV). Jesus says:

"Let not your heart be troubled: ye believe in God, believe also in me. In my Father's house are many mansions: if it were not so, I would have told you."

> To me, this is Jesus Christ standing upon the mountain on the planet and shouting to the entire world "trust me." Why is He shouting that? **Because everybody on the planet is going to leave their bodies "sooner or later" AND WHERE ARE YOU GOING TO GO?** Those who are connected to Him *are going where He is.* Now, when He mentions the word "house," this is what He's saying, "I'm trying to tell you how to

get to my Daddy's house. He's telling the entire world, "You want to get to my Daddy's house, *"this is the way to it!"* He's saying, "There's only one way and *it's through me!"* It's not *"the way it looks, it's the way it is!"* One of the things that I see happens with those who are born-again, we act like it's a belief system. It is so, whether we believe it or not. There's no other way! Sometimes, we don't want to offend somebody else's belief system or somebody else's religion. I'm telling you right now, it has nothing to do with belief; *it's the way it is!* There are people that don't believe in gravity. I could stand up all day and say, "I don't believe in gravity," but whether I believe in it or not, it's the way it is. And guess what? That's what, one day, everybody is going to find out. My Bible says, "Every knee is going to bow and every tongue is going to confess that Jesus Christ is Lord." It's better they find out now; because, on that day, it will be too late. You don't have to argue or debate with them; they'll all find out *"sooner or later."*

To me, people are trying to find various contrary statements to try to prove themselves right. The way I respond to this is "I don't have to be right; Jesus is." I just rely on His rightness. I'm going to tell you right now, even in Heaven you're not right; Jesus is. What's shining out of you is the righteousness of God. On the day that I went to Heaven, I went to His Father's house *because He said it!* Most of us don't realize that. We don't go because we said it; we go because He said it. I accepted Him as my Lord and Saviour (don't get me wrong), but He's the one who says whether I go in or not. I just did exactly what He said I was supposed to do, then it was out of my hands, because I was born-again. Because believing that you're going to Heaven is not what saves you, Jesus is! When I got to Heaven, I found out that many of the boxes that I had built for God were all wrong!

I have a degree in Pastoral Counseling with a theological background. When I went to Heaven, many boxes I had built for God were blown apart. But guess what? He didn't go outside His word. *HE WENT OUTSIDE "MY BOX," BUT "HE DIDN'T GO OUTSIDE HIS WORD!" The reason for that is that the word is "ALIVE <u>AND</u> LIVING," and it never stops moving! We may stop moving, but it never stops moving!*

DEAN SETS FRAMEWORKS FOR QUESTION AND ANSWER SESSION:

I'm going to put some frameworks around this session. I believe I'm on my way home and this is the journey that God said I need to go on, as I go home. So, I make myself as available, as possible, to answer these types of questions for anybody who wants to ask them. I don't know everything. I don't have to. I don't have to be right; Jesus does. I just rely on His rightness. I don't get you in Heaven; Jesus does. I never went to the Bible to look for the things I experienced in Heaven. However, I am an avid Bible reader, so when I would be reading the Bible, I would say, "Oh, there it is!" That's how it usually happens.

The other thing that helped is that my pastor read the Bible first in the Greek and then in the English. So, whenever I would have difficulty in identifying what I experienced in Heaven I would ask him about it, and he would tell me where it was found in the Scriptures. Many times, when

I had been taught where "we believed one way," but I had experienced it another way in Heaven; I would say to my pastor, "This is what I experienced." And he would usually say, "Well, that's the way the Greek Bible says it."

A good example would be this one: I wasn't told (by Jesus) that I couldn't say anything about my experience. God didn't tell me not to. From some people's interpretation of 2 Corinthians 12:4, they say Paul was told he couldn't say things about what he experienced in Heaven. And really what the Scripture meant by "it was unspeakable" (in the Greek) was that there was no reference inside of him, for him to be able to explain his experiences or describe them.

PASTOR'S COMMENT:

And that's the way I saw Paul's comment (even though I didn't know about the Greek), that he couldn't interpret or articulate what he experienced. It was nothing found in his language to express the concepts he saw.

DEAN'S COMMENT:

Not just because there were no words, but because there was no reference in his culture to describe what he saw. I like to use the example like this; if a person lived in the jungle and came to civilization and cut on the lights. Now they would try to go back to their culture and explain to their people what lights are and how they work. They may say the modernized people "have fire in the ceiling and a stick that they turn the fire on with."

They have nothing in their culture to explain this phenomenon to their people.

QUESTION: HOW DOES THE ETERNAL REALM vs. THE TEMPORAL REALM AFFECT YOUR RESPONSES?

DEAN'S RESPONSE:

So, when I'm trying to tell you about Heaven, I'm trying to tell you <u>in the five senses</u>. I'm trying to explain an eternal realm in a temporal realm. We say, "natural or supernatural realm." No. That's the eternal realm (pointing upwardly). This is the temporal realm (spreading hands somewhat downward). The Bible even says, "The things that you do not see are eternal; the things that you can see are temporal." And whether you realize it or not, *when you become born-again, you become an eternal being. And, it isn't that you <u>become eternal "now"</u> and when you get to Heaven <u>you "pick-up where you left off"</u> on earth. It's "altogether" (there's no interruption in your salvation).* The day you accepted Jesus as Lord and Saviour, "you <u>became an eternal being</u>!" Is that good news? And that's how God wants you to walk on this planet.

I can tell you what I heard, I can tell you what I experienced, but you would have had to have an experience with God to relate. *And, if you're born-again, you would have had to have that experience.* Most of us don't realize it; we can't explain to people in temporal words how that *"born-again"* experience took place within us. When you try to describe what it was like to be born-again, you can't "really say" anything! There are no words to describe what happened to you! The only reason I can relate to you is because it happened to me.

BEFORE CREATION, PLANET LIFE, AFTER LIFE

Someone who hasn't been born-again and know Jesus Christ can't relate!

Now, because of this conflict of eternal things versus temporal limitations <u>in the human five senses,</u> I can tell you what I saw in Heaven, but I like to say it was "like" this or that. I'm not saying that's what it is, but this is as close as I can get to describe the things I saw there. You know, the Bible does this too. In the book of Revelation, when John is describing things he saw, he says, "like crystal." Some people will come back from a NDE and say, "I saw a crystal sea," but John says, "like crystal." Ezekiel talks about his experience saying, "Like a wheel within a wheel." Daniel says, "like" a lot. They're doing the best they can to describe an eternal realm in a temporal realm, because, in fact, that's not what it is.

When I was in Heaven, I saw angels that looked like they had helicopter blades on their heads. That's what I would have said in the flesh, but the Bible calls it a "wheel within a wheel." A lot of times people don't realize that our flesh is always competing with our spirit, trying to describe spiritual things. When we are trying to describe the spiritual realm, the body wants to try to define it, rather than letting the Spirit do it. That's why I use the word of God, when I sense the flesh wanting to start telling me, "This is what you really saw" and "what you really experienced." A lot of times when your flesh gets involved, it will start trying to control the spirit realm. Your flesh can't control the spiritual realm, so you need the word of God; and you will literally have it the way the word of God says it. Then, we will have our answers line up with the way God says it. Because, if anybody knows about spiritual things, it's God.

Because of this dilemma, many NDEers come back and they are describing things of Heaven as though those things were in the earthly realm. And they're not! But that's the flesh trying to understand something that is in the eternal realm. That's your flesh doing it like that, because that's the best way that it could be described. Because the word for it is not on the planet.

Some people say, "Not everything God has done is in His word," and I will respond to that like this: When it said that all the books could not contain all the things that Jesus had done on the planet, it was really talking about 'books at that time.' We'll say all the books ever, and all the books at that time. However, we have more ability to capture more data than ever before. So, when the Scriptures said that, you could say, "Yeah, that's right." But the reality of this is that until you can tell me everything that is in the word, you can't really tell me it's not in there. And what happens, a lot of times, is that the person with this perspective won't take the time to search it out in the word. Ninety-nine percent of everything that I experienced when I went to be with the Father and Jesus, I could find Scripture for it in the word, and I would not be taking it out of context either.

Those of you who have experienced supernatural things, I would suggest that you say to God, "Now, God, I experienced this thing or that, now show me where I can see it in the word," and He'll show you. He'll show you some Scriptures and you may say to yourself afterward, "I never saw this in the word like this before." Sometimes, we look at Heavenly things from an earthly viewpoint, rather than an Heavenly viewpoint. And when God does show us things from an Heavenly viewpoint, we'll go to a commentary that a man or woman wrote, and we'll try to prove that God's right, instead of going back to the word of God.

QUESTION: DO WE EXPERIENCE TRANSFORMATION IN BITS AND PIECES? IS IT ALMOST LIKE (WHAT I SEE IS THAT) YOU EXPERIENCED TRANSFORMATION AS SOON AS YOU WENT TO HEAVEN? FOR EXAMPLE, YOU JUST STEPPED INTO IT!

DEAN'S RESPONSE:

> No. It was more of, "*I was already transformed and didn't know it!*" Because I always tell people, "When I got there (Heaven), I didn't have to be cleaned-up or go through a class to learn anything." I already knew it! So, this tells me that the day you become born-again, *it's already planted on the inside of you. It's already there!* I like to go to St. John where Jesus says, "I am the vine, and ye are the branches." (St. John 15:1) Whether we realize it or not, we are *already connected to Jesus and* everything *in His kingdom*. What happens is that your flesh stops you from really experiencing that connection.
>
> I used to try to talk about everything in Heaven, but now I feel like the best thing you can do is go yourself and find out. Some people ask me, "Why don't you talk about Heaven more?" And my response is, "Heaven doesn't get you in, Jesus does!" And that's why I spend a lot of time talking about Jesus. Because even though I was to spend

a lot of time talking about Heavenly things and trying to describe them, "I am way short!" It's better that you don't see it now, but rather that you experience it later. What I mean by that is, when you see a flower in Heaven, you don't just see a flower. You experience it, and you experience everything about the flower. You experience if the petals move. You experience the fluid moving through the petals (the life). And you're connected to everything and everything is connected to you. Other people question me saying, "Well, you couldn't have seen everything." My response is, "You don't need to. You're connected to everything there, and everything there is connected to you."

I find out that I usually get four (4) types of questions:

1. I usually get questions from little kids. They usually ask questions on the topic of "Is it going to be fun?" Because, they want to know if it's going to be fun. I had one kid ask me one time, "Does Jesus have a belly button?" I almost started crying, do you know why? If Jesus didn't have a belly button, if He didn't die on the cross (as a human being), I wouldn't have been there in Heaven.

2. Teenagers are usually asking in the realm of "Is that God as powerful as they say He is?" They want to know if we really have a powerful God. They're not blind from seeing what's going on in this world of ours. A lot of times, they're in to other things, because they're trying not to "see" what's going on.

3. The other area is usually from people around my age (between thirty to sixty or seventy) and have gone to church. Most of their questions go something like this, "I've built a box for God and I want to know if this is the right box?" I've got to say this to you, He blew a ton of my boxes apart, but He didn't go outside of His word. Ninety-nine percent of almost everything I experienced, (and I experienced some stuff), you can find in the word of God. As you notice, when I'm sharing something, I tell you where it is in the Scriptures. And the reason for that is not to prove that I'm right (because I'm telling you I'm "way short"), but if you go to Acts Chapter 10 and read it, He'll show you even more.

4. And the last area of questions is from the elderly. Most of the questions that come from the elderly are similar to the children. They know they're closer to being home and they just want to know, "What's it going to be like?"

[THE QUESTION AND ANSWER SESSION BEGINS]

QUESTION: WHAT DID IT FEEL LIKE TO DIE (OR TAKE YOUR LAST BREATH)?

ANSWER FROM PASTOR:

(Can I share something I believe God spoke into my spirit concerning this?) I recall asking God how it would feel for me to take my last breath and He spoke this to me. He asked me if I could remember how it felt to take my first breath (after coming out of my mother's womb)? He asked if I could recall any physical reaction to that first breath, and I said "No." Then He said, "And that's the same way it's going to be when you take your last."

DEAN'S RESPONSE:

Yes. And, matter-of-fact, when the body takes that last breath, you're not there! You're not even in the body, when *"the body"* is breathing its last breath. A lot of people think someone is still there and the person is already gone. This is what happens, sometimes, in that last moment, people go back and forth, back and forth. They'll go to Heaven for a while, and then they go back and forth. They'll go to Heaven and have that "out-of-body" experience first, before leaving permanently.

When your husband (Richard) died and when he came back to life that first time, he was an eternal being. He knew he didn't die (an eternal death).

PASTOR:

Yes. I can recall that his consciousness (spirit and soul) was still "alive" when he had his near-death experience, because he described to me that "everything went from dark to darker," before we prayed him back to this life. This makes me realize that if he died like we have been taught to believe ("everything stops"), then his consciousness would have stopped also. Now I understand that he was "still alive;" it was only his body that died or "stopped." (Jesus said, "he that liveth and believeth in me shall never die).

DEAN'S RESPONSE:

So, here is what happened to me. Well, my heart stopped for one hour and forty-five minutes. Really what happened to me was this, I died. I can't tell you what it's like to die for a person who doesn't know Christ. I can only tell you what it's like to die for the person who does know Christ. That's the only thing I can do. I can't tell you anything outside of that.

I can remember them wheeling me down the hallway, after the operation. My wife said I was in recovery for three hours (extra longer than I should have been in there). I remember thinking to myself, *"I can't breathe." "I'm getting shallower and shallower breaths."* All of a sudden, what rose up inside of me was, "I am dying!" I'm thinking, *"How come I'm dying, when I came into the hospital for kidney stones. No, I didn't sign up for this!"*

From this experience, I have come to understand something, when it comes upon you, you know it's going to happen. When that day comes, when you're supposed to leave this planet to be with the Father and Jesus, *you're not going to be surprised!* It's going to come upon you. I believe it comes with the package.

I can remember thinking to myself, *"That was the worst way for me to die,"* because I can remember almost drowning. As a little boy, I jumped into a pool of water and almost drowned, and I remembered what it was like to go under and having water come into my lungs. And I remember saying to God (just me and God in conversation), "If I'm going to die, please don't let it be suffocating." And here I am suffocating; my lungs just shutting down and I couldn't get the air inside that I needed to be able to breathe. I thought when that moment came upon me I'd be hysterical, panicking, freaked-out, and yet, when it came upon me when I was dying (all of a sudden), something rose up inside me and I said, "I'm going home!" That's what I said. I don't know about your husband, but if anybody had laid hands on me to stop me, at that moment, I would have been mad.

"I didn't freak-out, I had peace, joy, and comfort. Everything that I thought would have happened, didn't happen. It comes with the package! *THIS IS THE IMPORTANT THING THAT PEOPLE NEED TO KNOW ABOUT WHAT IT'S LIKE TO DIE from natural causes or accidents.* Whenever I am asked this question, I respond, I don't know. I wasn't there! I had already left! Most of us don't understand this. It isn't that the body dies, *IT'S THAT THE SPIRIT LEAVES! IT'S THAT THE SPIRIT LEAVES and THEN THE BODY DIES!* Where's that in the Bible? "For the body without the spirit is dead ...."" (James 2:26)

You may have had a loved one, and you said you saw them *"WHEN THEY TOOK THEIR LAST BREATH."* No. You just saw the last of the gas run out of the car. It comes with the package. Even if they are involved in terrible accidents, *THEY LEFT THEIR BODIES BEFORE IT HAPPENED! THEY WEREN'T THERE!* Most people don't realize that.

"In Hebrews 2:14–15, the Bible says that Jesus took part in our death to destroy its fear and power over us. Most of the time we think it is only speaking about our spiritual death, but it's also speaking about our physical death. He died our physical death; He endured our pain. He took the pain, at that moment of dying, that we were supposed to be experiencing. How do I know that? In the Scripture, Apostle Paul wrote that there *was no longer A STING IN DEATH!" (1 Corinthians 15:55–56)*

DEAN'S RESPONSE TO PASTOR:

That's why when you read those books written by those NDEers, and they said they couldn't tell how it felt to die, it is because they weren't there. I don't know what it was like to suffocate, because I wasn't there! And I didn't turn around to look back! Most of us don't realize that. We leave our bodies. It comes with the package!

When I was at the feet of Jesus I was thanking Him, and I said, "You did this for me." The first thing I was thanking Him for was that **"HE DIED MY DEATH!"** I didn't get up there and say, "Hey, I thought we had an understanding of 'no suffocation'." You've got to let go of it! They're not complaining up in Heaven! Let it go! We've got work to do down here!

You know what's sad about this gift Jesus gave to us of dying the Christian's death? Those who refuse to know Him as Lord and Saviour, they've got to go through that physical pain and death, *even though He already died (or paid) for it.* Is that sad or is that sad? You know how I know that, because when I left, I left my body here. It was my spirit and my soul that went up to Heaven. The spirit and soul, they don't die!

QUESTION: DOES YOUR CONSCIENCE HAVE ANY REMEMBRANCE OF THE FEELING OF LEAVING YOUR BODY?

DEAN'S RESPONSE:

> Again, let's acknowledge the Scripture that says, "He that liveth and believeth in me shall never die." (St. John 11:26) Since your spirit and soul never dies, **you don't have any remembrance of** *"what really* **DID *NOT HAPPEN*. BECAUSE YOU DID NOT DIE, THEREFORE, YOUR CONSCIOUSNESS *IS NEVER INTERRUPTED; IT REMAINS IN TACT!*** You only take with you the good things in your consciousness when you die/sleep. We don't take bad things. We only take the good. God wanted me to emphasize to you that you walk on the planet now as a being that never dies. You're eternal now!

QUESTION: WHAT FORM DO WE TAKE WHEN WE GET TO HEAVEN?

DEAN'S RESPONSE:

> When Jesus showed up on the Mount. Transfiguration, Moses and Elijah showed up *after they had been to Heaven (or paradise)*. The disciples could recognize them, because they had a form. You will have everything that you have now; head, eyes, mouth, nose, arms, hands, legs, feet.

QUESTION: SINCE WE WILL HAVE A NOSE, WILL WE NEED TO BREATHE UP THERE?

DEAN'S RESPONSE:

No. You don't need air there. You live off of Jesus. (Even, here, we're supposed to live off of Jesus.) Remember when Jesus said, "I have food (meat) that you know not of?" See, after my experience, I knew what He meant from the Scriptures. Yes, you still have form. God didn't make a mistake when He made you. The form that you're in right now (i.e. what you look like) is the form that will remain. When God created you, He didn't make any mistakes. I even tell people to get used to this face, because you'll see it forever. You are eternal beings to the extent that the body or form that we are in, it defines our physical looks, and when the body dies, the spirit and soul leaves, but it will retain the same form. You keep your identity that you had on this planet. *The reason your form looks like it does now, is because it is deteriorating. What will it look like when it is "not" deteriorating?* Most of us have never considered this phenomenon. Some NDEers say, "You'll look young." No. "You'll look better than young, because there's *"no" old and deteriorating there!* You must have something "old" to compare it to by calling *something else "young;"* and there's nothing "old" in Heaven. See, what happened was that we were put into a body that lives on this planet and it deteriorates, but you still have a form. In Heaven, you're not limited like that any longer. And because of time, we grow (and that's a whole different thing happening to our bodies). Do you understand what I'm talking about?

What used to amaze me, when I came back, is we always think it's our minds that move our body, and after my experience, I realized that it is our spirit that moves our body. And I would think "man" as light as it is (and it's very light compared to how it moves this heavy body); that's what I was thinking. It was amazing to me, to see that happening.

QUESTION: SOME NDEers SAY THEY SMELLED SWEET AROMAS IN HEAVEN

DEAN'S RESPONSE:

I can't tell you, accurately, how Heaven smells, and I can't tell you how it tastes. AND THERE IS A SMELL AND TASTE IN HEAVEN. The reason is, there's something here that's not there *and it's called "death."* Nothing is falling apart up there. Nothing is decaying there. Nothing is dying there.

I know some people say, "Well, it smelled like flowers." Some say, "A sweet scent." But even if you say that, you've got to understand something. There's something *in the air (here) all the time and it's called "decay" and "death."* Whether you realize it or not, you've gotten used to the smell. *It's in the air right now!* So, I can't tell you what the "Heavenly" smell is like, because there really is no way to describe it here. Because, again, here we have death and decay happening around us all the time. Where you really have it stand out is when you go to a hospital, and most of us don't like to go to hospitals, because you're smelling "decay" and "death." Nursing home—"decay" and "death." Outhouse—"decay" and "death." In Heaven, there's no "decaying." There's nothing "dying." The most I can do, is ask God to give this understanding to you, because I'm having a hard time trying to tell people what it was "like." Because, again, there's really no way to describe it here (on this planet). Since I can't describe what it's like, I use the word of God and, by the Holy Spirit, He will give you more.

Now, when I say that, you might say, "AW, that's great," but I'm saying, He really wants you to know more. And I'm not saying it because it sounds good. I'm saying, if you're in this room, hearing my voice right now, and He gives you a Scripture, it's because He wants you to know more.

QUESTION: DID THEY HAVE MUSIC IN HEAVEN, COLOR, AND SO FORTH? WHAT WAS IT LIKE?

DEAN'S RESPONSE:

One of the things I'm going to say now, is that I'm going to be going a little bit deeper (as I call it); "into the veins." When I was there, we were all before the Father praising Him. There was a moment where everything in Heaven was called around the throne of God to give Him praise and glory, and to sing to Him. Then He would sing back to us—each and every one of us, He sang love songs to. And it was a personal love song for us. And He could do it all at the same time, because He's God. So, He could sing to you and (at the same time) sing to me. I really do believe that during praise and worship time, when you feel the presence of God over you, *that's God singing over you!* And here we are, literally, singing to Him *and Him singing back to us!* It's almost like the Song of Solomon.

That type of exchange. He's telling you how much He loves you, and you're telling Him how much you love Him. And you have a new thing (expression) all the time. Something new is always there. So, during that time frame, when He would be singing back to us; when we would sing, the water would go up and *wrap around the songs that were going up to Him!* Almost like instruments. Almost like the water was playing the song. Remember, I'm not saying it is, I'm saying "like," because that's the best way I can describe it. Everything is alive there; nothing's dead; everything's got life; the grass, the flowers, the water, and the liquid. Everything is living!

And another thing, the colors that were coming down from the Father, *they would really come "around the song" that you were singing and dance and go on back up to the Father!* So, everything would interact with your praise or your worship that you were giving to the Father. **But when the Father sung to us, nothing got in between His love flowing from Him to us—nothing got in the way! Everything got out of the way!** And it was like I knew that the Lord Jesus Christ loved us! I just didn't know how much. There was no way to put into any boundaries of how much He loved us. But I came to realize that the *FATHER'S LOVE IS "ENORMOUS,"* because when He got to me, nothing got in the way! Nothing was going to stop His love from reaching me, no matter what!

QUESTION: DID MUSIC HAVE A RHYTHM? OR BECAUSE OF IT EXISTING IN "ETERNITY" OR BEING IN A PLACE OF "TIMELESSNESS," WAS THE MUSIC AFFECTED BY THAT KIND OF ATMOSPHERE?

PASTOR'S RESPONSE:

One musician, who had a NDE, said he didn't hear timing like our music beats on the planet.

DEAN'S RESPONSE:

I'm not a musician, so I don't have a lot of the background for that. There was music there, but there was a beat that was different from any I have ever experienced. There was singing. I was there when everything came together to worship or give praise to the Father. I do remember that *music is "alive,"* and so, it's not just that *"singing is alive."* Even now, when we give God praise, *our "music is alive" too!* Most people don't realize that! And because we don't realize that fact, we don't give it all that we have into it! However, your spirit always wants to praise or worship the Lord. If people would let go, and not listen to the flesh, and say, "This day I'm going to give praise, whether my flesh wants to or not," they would have a whole different experience in the spirit. But your spirit always wants to praise God—the real you!

QUESTION: WHAT WAS COMMUNICATION LIKE BETWEEN PEOPLE?

DEAN'S RESPONSE:

When I was with the Father and Jesus, no one spoke. No words were spoken. If anything was said, it was always said in song. Most communication is thought-to-thought. For example, if I was going to talk about this book, instead of me talking about it, I would just give (or send) you the picture. I'm not going to verbally describe it to you. I'm not going to tell you it's so many feet tall or how wide it is. I'm just going to give it to you and move on. That's what the communication would be like.

Also, you don't just see with your eyes. *YOU SEE WITH EVERYTHING YOU WERE CREATED OF.* So, when God talks about things in His word and says "see," He's not just saying "see" in the sense of looking or seeing with your eyes. In Heaven, you're seeing it with everything you're created of (your entire being). *You don't "see" it. You "experience it." Seriously, you "experience it."*

QUESTION: YOU SAID THAT THERE WAS NO COMMUNICATION WITH YOUR MOUTHS, BUT ONLY PICTURES. WAS THAT ALWAYS?

DEAN'S RESPONSE:

When I communicated or anything was communicated to me, it was thought-to-thought. The only thing that Jesus said to me was, "No. It's not your time. Go back." Everything else He did was thought-to-thought. Almost like downloading from a computer, or that type of thing.

QUESTION: LIKE A VISION?

DEAN'S RESPONSE:

Well, if we're going to talk about vision, I'm going to give it to you in a picture. That's how God talks to us now. Most people don't hear an audible voice from God. God just talks to you in your thoughts. The bottom line is, when I was there (everything that opened its mouth, when it opened its mouth), it was in song. Even the Bible, if you read the King James Version, it will say, "They spoke this or that." The New Translation will say that, "They sung this or that." Because the word that it goes back to can be translated to singing or speaking. But because the translators would sometimes think, "Okay, they must be speaking instead of singing," *then they wrote* "speaking instead of singing."

PASTOR'S COMMENT: **THE BOOKS I READ SAID THAT THE INFORMATION WAS SHARED "FAST" OR AT AN "UNIMAGINABLE" SPEED.**

DEAN'S RESPONSE:

Again, we're trying to explain it in this realm, and we're trying to put that explanation into these words we have here. So, "fast" is not even a concept there. And you're not able to describe speed. If I was to send a thought to my wife, it would be "whooosh!" We wouldn't be talking about speed or how fast we're speaking. We're trying to do that, because we're on the planet. But the reality of it is *"the way"* we communicate.

When I came back to this planet, one of the things I had a hard time with was that I would talk inside myself thinking I talked to you. When I thought I talked to my wife, I never did, because I had become accustomed to that type of communication up there.

QUESTION: IN YOUR EXPERIENCE, YOU SAID YOU SAW GENERATIONS BACK. HOW DID YOU KNOW THAT?

DEAN'S RESPONSE:

> You just know! It's almost like on Mount. Transfiguration, when Moses and Elijah were talking to Jesus, and you had the disciples there. They knew who Moses and Elijah were. They recognized them. Well, those were family members. You understand, you don't see, anymore, by sight, only. In Heaven you don't see by sight only. You see by everything that you are. Here on the planet, we view things by our eyesight.

QUESTION: DO WE RECEIVE NEW NAMES IN HEAVEN?

DEAN'S RESPONSE:

> Someone asked me recently, whether God gave me a new name in Heaven. Some of you have already been given the name that God wanted you to have, because your parents went to God and He gave them a name. A lot of us don't know that when God calls us, He doesn't call us by the name that we have; He calls us by the name that He has given us. It's because your name is your purpose. And, if He calls you by your purpose, nothing will return unto Him void—you're going to accomplish what you're supposed to accomplish.

QUESTION: DOES HE CALL US BY OUR NAMES AS WE'RE IN THE PROCESS?

DEAN'S RESPONSE:

> No. He calls us by our names as a completion. The Scripture I would go to for confirmation of this is when Gideon was hiding from the enemy, God didn't say, "You're going be a mighty man of war." He said, (called him right out), "Mighty man of valor."

QUESTION: HOW DOES YOUR SPIRIT/SOUL KNOW THE WAY TO HEAVEN?

DEAN'S RESPONSE:

> "Some people believe that angels or family members are sent to escort you home. You don't need angels to bring you home. You don't need family members to bring you home. *You don't even need Jesus to bring you home!* Apostle John says, "You know the way!"" (St. John 14:6)
>
> When I left my body, I didn't have an angel *standing there*. Someone asked, "Was there someone standing there?" I said, "If they were, I left them behind, because *I KNEW THE WAY.*" There was no star up in the atmosphere to direct me, in the sense that I was to be sure to make a left turn or right turn. No. *YOU KNOW THE WAY!*

QUESTION: HOW FAST DID YOU TRAVEL THROUGH SPACE?

DEAN'S RESPONSE:

When I left this body, how long did it take to get into God's presence? How long did it take *to leave this body* and be in the presence of the Lord? Apostle Paul said, "…to be absent from the body, and be present with the Lord." (2 Corinthians 5:8) My answer to this is, "*FASTER* than you could even blink; by the time your top eyelid can hit the bottom, I was there." *FASTER* than you're hearing my voice. *FASTER* than the light is shining down from the ceiling on your face.

I can remember leaving that hospital room, and I can remember leaving through the blue sky, going into outer space, and going into this space called **"the outer darkness (there's nothing there but darkness),"** but when I was in it, (and I was headed toward the **"window,"**) it looked more like a window to me, although some say it's a light, a tunnel. The best way I can describe it is a **"window."**

As I was headed toward that window, I can remember seeing (all of a sudden) lights pass me by. They looked like shooting stars, but you know what they were? They were the prayers that people were praying for me and prayers that people were praying for others. These prayers were getting there before me. And how fast was I moving?

That means, if you had given me a head start on that day, May 5, 2006, and you started praying, your prayers would have beat me there! You know why that is? Because the Father "wants" to hear from you. *You were "made" to talk to Him!* That which we are, which is a spiritual being, always wants to talk to its daddy. It's our flesh that doesn't want this to happen. Understand that most of our problems are not with the devil, however, we blame most of them on him. But it's our own flesh. And the Bible tells us what or where our battle comes from; lust of the eye, lust of the flesh and the pride of life. These are those issues which get us into trouble. Then Satan comes along and grabs those things and goes along with them, but it's your flesh, people!

Do you know what my flesh said when I got back here? While I was lying in bed thinking about the things of Heaven, my flesh said to me, "You will never do that to me again!" And you know what I said? "You're a lie!" The Bible tells you about your carnality. Your carnal mind battles against your spiritual thinking! A lot of times, we try to get our flesh to come in line and think it's going to come and go along with the Spirit.

QUESTION: SHOULD WE WALK (TOTALLY) AS ETERNAL BEINGS?

PASTOR:

I recall reading a book by a NDEer who was an atheist prior to his Heavenly experience. And he said he now believes that every Christian should walk as though they have one foot on this planet and the other in Heaven.

DEAN'S RESPONSE:

Well, for me it's different, and I'll just share it with you. I believe, once we become born-again, we become eternal beings, so we should walk as though we are always in the eternal realm; not as though we are in the temporal realm.

So, like the NDEer is saying, "Walk with one foot on earth and one in Heaven;" I can't go there, because I don't want to have one foot off and one foot on. I want to walk on this planet as an eternal being on my way home. And that means, today, the fruit of the spirit will operate in me, whether I want them to or not. I'm going to love you, whether I want to or not. I'm going to be kind to you, whether I want to or not. Because a lot of times, when we say we've got one foot on the planet and one foot in Heaven, that's a means to justify the foot on the planet. We'll start justifying that way of doing things, because we have got one foot on this planet. That's not the way Jesus did it! He didn't have one foot on the planet and one in Heaven. He was human, but He was an eternal being. You see, you're eternal and Heaven is your realm. When the Bible said, "You're seated in Heavenly places with Christ Jesus," God does not see you here on the planet. He sees you there!

QUESTION: DID THE FATHER SHOW YOU THE THRONE? DID YOU SEE CHERUBIMS AND SERAPHIMS WORSHIPPING AROUND THE THRONE? DID YOU SEE THE FATHER IN HIS GLORY?

COMMENT:

I know you said you saw Jesus, but I didn't know if you saw the Father (the Spirit).

DEAN'S RESPONSE:

Yes. I saw the Father.

COMMENT:

Wow!

DEAN'S RESPONSE:

> Most of the time, we remember the story in Exodus where God told Moses, "Thou canst not see my face: for there shall no man see me and live." (Exodus 33:20) And, he had to experience God from behind a rock (see His hinder parts). Well, that was because Moses was in the flesh (at that time) and not in spirit form. The Apostle John saw Him in the spirit; Daniel saw Him in the spirit; and Ezekiel saw Him in the spirit. They got to see Him when they also became spirit, like Him (their spirit form).

QUESTION: WHEN YOU SAY, "IN THE SPIRIT," HELP ME UNDERSTAND *EXACTLY* WHAT YOU MEAN.

DEAN'S RESPONSE:

> It's the flesh that cannot handle seeing God and live.

QUESTION: AND YOU GOT TO SEE HIM?

DEAN'S RESPONSE:

> Oh, yeah! Most of us don't realize that. He would not hide Himself from us! We're His children. He looks at us as His children. We don't understand

the magnitude of that! It's like anybody who has a child; you look at them differently than you look at other people. They have a different level in your life. Well, He looks at us as His children. He doesn't look at us as a human being, He doesn't look at you as a man or a woman. He looks at you as His child. And, He wants you to "behold" His face! That's correct! He made you to be able to look at Him. Adam looked at Him, before he messed up, remember (in the Garden) everyday? It was after Adam messed up that he could no longer look at Him. But before that, He looked at Him.

QUESTION: WHEN YOU'RE IN HEAVEN, DO YOU SEE WHAT'S GOING ON IN THE EARTH REALM?

DEAN'S RESPONSE:

When the Apostle John was in Heaven, in the Book of Revelation, he got to look down on the planet several times. Are you ready for this? You know, we say John looked at the past, the present, and the future. In Heaven, there is no past, present, and future. Everything is now! He looked at it *AS NOW*. A lot of times that's why people have a hard time reading the Book of Revelation. It is because they're trying to put it in a timeline. And John didn't even see it in a timeline. He saw it *IN THE NOW!* Interesting, Huh? But anytime you go into the spiritual realm, you never see it in a timeline. You see it in the now.

I don't know why God is letting me share all these things with you all. Most places I go, I don't get to share it like this. I'm just letting you know. My wife will tell you, it's usually never like this. But

He's really letting me go into some of the veins of some of the spiritual things I experienced. The "veins." You know, like the veins in your body? That's where I'm going—in depth—the veins. The very life that flows through them.

See, my job, a lot of times, is just like walking down a hallway and opening doors. Then light starts coming through their doors. And, I tell people, "If light comes through that door, and you get attracted to that light, you should go through that door, because God is saying, 'You need more.'" I can go there and say, "This is what I'm doing. I'm just opening doors. 'I'm on my way home.'" But everybody who is born-again, knows the Lord and Saviour, and Holy Spirit-filled, you're on your way home too!

QUESTION: YOU MENTIONED EARLIER, THAT MANY OF THE "BOXES" YOU HAD FOR GOD, HE BLEW AWAY.

DEAN:

Yes, He did; but He never went "outside of His word." What I meant by that is "This is what I believe; this is what I think it is." I got to Heaven and, whooosh: it's all blown apart! And then I go to the word and I say, "Oh, that's what it said in the Bible." That's what I'm saying. For example, St. John 10:9 says that we find green pastures on both sides. And in the next verse, Jesus talks about doors. That's that spiritual realm. You can find pastures on both sides, and you can "go in and out." Does that make sense to you? Read it again, with that thinking in mind. Because, now, what I opened up for you, those Scriptures will take on a different meaning. It's not talking natural or temporal; it's talking spiritual. You're experiencing that Scripture. That's what you're experiencing.

QUESTION: WHY DO YOU BELIEVE NDE EXPERIENCES RELIEVE PEOPLE FROM THE FEAR OF DEATH?

DEAN:

One of the reasons I really believe that God has me to emphasize that "we don't die," and that we just leave our body and "our body dies" (but we don't die), is so that we can do the things that He wants us to do. Because, a lot of times, He literally asks us to go into situations where *death* might be a part of what we may have to deal with. And I've seen physical death, but sometimes it's your reputation that may have to die. You may have to do something but knowing that you do not have the fear that that thing "does not kill you."

The Lord told me to emphasize on what it is like to die, as a Christian. History says that, "Paul *RAN TOWARD THE CHOPPING BLOCK!!*" Because Paul said in Scripture, "To die is gain, but to live on the planet is for you." Prophet Agabus (by the Spirit) warned him but couldn't change his mind. The Lord let Paul make the final decision.

QUESTION: DO YOU THINK PAUL'S EXPERIENCE IN 2 CORINTHIANS 12:4 CAUSED HIM NOT TO FEAR?

DEAN'S RESPONSE:

Most people who realize that they don't die will put themselves in situations which others would think are crazy. Do you understand what I mean? I remember, right after this experience happened to me, I was just lost. I can remember a couple of times or a few incidences that kind of brought this out. It was when my wife and I were flying for the first time. We were flying to Cleveland, and as we got closer to Cleveland, the plane began to rock around, and it dropped. And everybody in the plane was screaming and hollering (and those kinds of things), and I was over there thinking, *"If this plane goes down, I go up!"* That's what I was thinking! I wasn't fearful!

DEAN'S QUESTION TO US: SO, WHAT'S THE WORST THING THAT CAN HAPPEN TO YOU PHYSICALLY?

AUDIENCE'S ANSWER:

Dying!

DEAN'S QUESTION: AND WHERE DO YOU GO?

AUDIENCE'S ANSWER:

Heaven!

DEAN'S RESPONSE:

So, we need to know this now, more than ever. We need to be the children of God that we're supposed to be, and walk that way, then we would have no fear. And to do that, we have to walk as *eternal beings*. When I left my body, the next step I took was in Heaven with the Father. This step was here, yes, but the next step was with my Father.

DEAN'S QUESTION TO US: WAS THERE A TRANSITION?

DEAN'S ANSWER:

No. I was just there!

QUESTION: WHAT'S YOUR VIEW ON PEOPLE WHO TAKE THEIR OWN LIVES?

DEAN'S RESPONSE:

If you do things like drugs or smoke, it tears your body up; it shortens your time. When you don't do something that is supposed to be healthy, it shortens your time. And we have a lot to do with other people's time being shortened on this planet, too.

PASTOR'S COMMENT:

Some situations, like when we don't intercede on someone's behalf, are also reasons for their time being shortened on this planet. For example, like your wife interceded for you. Sometimes, we should have stopped the hand of death, because God wanted it for His glory and for their blessing. I had one Bishop who spoke and said that, when we get to Heaven, we're going be made aware that lots of people should not have gone home prematurely. I don't believe God's going to punish us for it but those persons might not have finished their assignments on the planet.

DEAN'S RESPONSE:

Yes. The disappointment in them being prematurely there, when God needed them here. Even abortions. I'm not getting down on anybody who had an abortion, but we took people out of the mix, who had answers for many of the issues that we have on the planet, right now. If a person leaves before their time, you have just taken them out of the mix for what they should have been doing (and was created to do) <u>or</u> they took themselves off the planet before their time. Then there's that gap there. (The harvest is great, but the laborers are few.) The reality of it is that, everybody is put here on this planet for a reason (to get somebody else to know Jesus Christ as Lord and Saviour). And it isn't that I don't think, if you went home, that God wouldn't have had someone else to reach out to a certain person. But, that person might have come to know Jesus Christ at the age of twenty-four instead of forty-four. And they might not have had to go through a whole lot of unnecessary issues, had they known Jesus as Saviour before getting to the age of forty-four.

When Jesus said to me, "No. It's not your time," I really believe He was saying, "I need you there more than I need you here." And, I believe that for every born-again Christian on the planet. It wasn't just my assignment; it was for us all! He needs you here. You've got work to do!

QUESTION: <u>HOW DO YOU FEEL ABOUT DEATH SEPARATING FAMILIES?</u>

<u>DEAN'S RESPONSE:</u>

After coming back from my experience, I don't like people being separated because of death. All the other issues people have, they are going to outlive. My responsibility, a lot of times, when talking to someone, is to try to infuse that life that they have lost, so that they can overcome whatever they've been going through. Then, they can fulfill what God has created them to accomplish on this planet. I don't like death. I just don't like it. I know how much pain it brings people, because of the separation. I know that they will be reunited together in Heaven, but we were never meant to be fragmented (i.e. broken apart) or separated.

I'll repeat, that we were never intended to be separated from each other (family). We were created to be together forever.

PASTOR'S COMMENT:

We were never supposed to be separated from God, in the first place, even though He let us come here in this body on this planet.

DEAN'S RESPONSE:

Adam messed up and sin came into the planet and now we have to be separated. It's like a whole piece of paper being ripped apart. That's what's going on there. The good thing about it, though, is that Jesus Christ came that we can be reunited together and never separated again. Do you know what God's desire is right now? It's that we will make sure that everybody we know is told something about Jesus. Our loved ones in Heaven want all their family members with them.

I also know the grieving process is a process to make you heal in that area. So, I don't look at it the same way as most people would look at it.

QUESTION: HOW DO YOU FEEL THE FRUIT OF THE SPIRIT IS APPROPRIATE FOR ETERNAL BEINGS?

DEAN'S RESPONSE:

I go to a lot of places where people say they are spiritual. And they show me love. They'll show me gentleness. They'll show me goodness, but faithfulness? No. Do you know that's part of the fruit of the Spirit? When is it supposed to be enacted? When you don't feel like doing things we should be doing.

There's a culture in Heaven, like we say here on earth, we have a culture. Guess where it starts? The day when you receive Him as Lord and Saviour, all the fruit of the Spirit is in the culture. Do you think you're going to get to Heaven and you're not going to love? The same for gentleness and self-control? Remember, you still have choices. You can make choices, if you want; you've just got to make the right choices. There won't be any flesh up there to try to influence you the wrong way. You might as well start doing it here, because you are going to have to do it forever, anyway. *EVERYBODY YOU COME IN CONTACT WITH, AND WHO ARE BORN-AGAIN, YOU WILL KNOW FOREVER! WE WILL ALWAYS KNOW EACH OTHER!*

You won't even talk about this moment in Heaven. They're eternal moments. Do you want this backed-up by Scripture? Go to Acts 10:1–40 where it speaks about the alms that Cornelius gave to others.

Some of you need to get a bigger memorial up in Heaven (seriously). *THE THINGS YOU DO*

FOR GOD "ARE ETERNAL;" THEY'RE NOT TEMPORAL! You see, there's no waste in Heaven! When I was there (how long, I don't know); if I was there only five minutes, every moment was like a universe. Nothing is wasted; everything has a meaning and it's something that goes on for eternity. That's God! *SO, THOSE THINGS THAT YOU DO FOR GOD, THEY'RE ETERNAL! NOTHING IS WASTED!*

PASTOR'S COMMENT:

One of the things I told my church was about the incident when the Bishop, where I was a member, died and his son succeeded him. I wanted to leave, like so many others were doing. So, I talked to my husband about us going to this Prophetic Conference to get direction as to where we should change our membership. Well, we got "a word," alright, but it was "a word" telling us to "Go back to that church and stay there, because that is where God wants to use you," and "people are watching you there!" I cried until the tears wet my shoes, along with making a puddle on the floor. We went back to that church and stayed ten more years. But most of all, we were faithful that entire time, because we knew that we had a mandate from God. Therefore, our faithfulness was directed more toward God than the pastor, even though the pastor benefited from it.

Then, during one of his first (beginning of the year) Consecration services, his theme was, "Stay Connected." And, as he was teaching on the different areas of our Christian dedication (or service) to the Lord that needed improving or correcting. Well, as he did, I was listening and making my mental notes of how I measured up to his requirements. And I proceeded to give myself "a pat" on the back, and before I could finish, the Holy Spirit invaded my thoughts with this question, "But what about the attitude in which you're doing those things?" It was like a dam broke loose in my chest and I began to weep, because the Holy Spirit had gone further than my "outward" workings and exposed "the intent" or attitude of my heart. I contacted him a few days later and repented "for the attitude of my heart."

DEAN'S RESPONSE:

As I stated earlier, as I was going into Heaven, all of a sudden, the prayers of the Saints for me and others were passing me by. They were going to the Father and Jesus, and when I came into Heaven, everything was right. Nothing was wrong. I came to understand something. *YOUR PRAYERS DON'T HAVE A "SHELF LIFE" (a use by date)*. Some of you are still in this room, because someone prayed for you generations ago. You're not just praying to anybody; *YOU'RE PRAYING TO GOD! HE'S ETERNAL! GOD IS STILL OPERATING OFF THEIR PRAYERS, AND THAT'S WHY YOU'RE STILL IN THIS ROOM.*

Do you know you were created to be in righteousness? That's why you have a hard time with wrongness. It's like someone trying to put a square peg into a round hole. You weren't created for doing wrong; *you* were created for rightness. I have written a book about Heaven, but if you really want to know about Heaven, you can read about it in the word; it's all there! That's why I use the word of God, a lot of times, when I explain the things I experienced with the Father and Jesus.

QUESTION: WHY DO YOU SAY, "THE FATHER AND JESUS" IN YOUR RESPONSES?

DEAN'S RESPONSE:

Someone asked me, one time, "Why do you always say, the Father and Jesus, and you don't say the Holy Spirit?" It's because the 'Holy Spirit' was "inside" me. The day that you are born-again, you "have the Holy Spirit" on the "*INSIDE OF YOU FOREVER" (EVEN WHEN YOUR SPIRIT LEAVES YOUR BODY)! YOU MAY AS WELL GET USED TO IT!* He said He'd never leave you nor forsake you, and when I got there (Heaven), *HE DIDN'T JUMP OUTSIDE OF ME AND SAY, "I've got to go get somebody else, now."* We hear some people saying, "Oh, the presence of God is here, *because I feel it!"* The presence of God is here, *because "He said"* He would be here! Whether you *"feel Him or not,"* He's here! Other people will say, *"Well, I don't 'feel' close to God."* It has nothing to do with your feelings. It has everything to do with what He said. He said He would never leave you nor forsake you! Yet, others will say, *"I've got to get closer to Him."* He's on the inside of you. How much closer can He get? If there's somebody in this room, right now, and you have done some things that are wrong, all you have to do is ask Him to forgive you, and He will. And some others of you play the game, sometimes, and *"act like you can walk away from*

Him, like He's not there, but He's there!" And you say, *"I hope He didn't hear that!"* He's on the inside listening to everything you say! *"I hope He didn't see that!"* He's on the inside of you! Just ask Him to forgive you and get back to work.

Also, I always acknowledged the Father and Jesus because the Bible says that, "God so loved the world that he gave his only begotten Son…" But then it really hit me. *LOVE WAS THERE "BEFORE" JESUS!* Before the Son was sent, He loved us! And I'm going to say something, and I'm saying it, because I want you to understand what the magnitude of being a child of God really means. What if Jesus, for some reason, didn't follow through with what He was supposed to do? We all know that when He went to the Garden of Gethsemane, He had a choice, because He said, "Not my will, but thine be done."

Remember that? He could have chosen something else. But, if He would not have done what the Father said, the Father would have found another way to redeem us. That's how powerful it is to be a child of God. He wants us! When you were formed inside of your mother, you were formed to have a fellowship with the Father. It's more intimate and constant to have fellowship with someone, rather than a relationship. A relationship is someone meeting with someone else, every once in a while. Whereas, a fellowship is when you spend time with an individual.

Chapter 8

THE PLACE CALLED HELL

WEBSTER'S DEFINITION: HELL-SHEOL—IN THE OLD TESTAMENT, "A PLACE" IN THE DEPTHS OF THE EARTH "WHERE THE DEAD ARE SUPPOSED TO GO;" "UNDERWORLD."

Revelation 1:18 gives another one of Jesus's missions for coming to earth and dying on Calvary, and that was to apprehend the "keys of hell and of death." The definition in the dictionary for "keys" is:

1. To secure or guard;
2. Something regarded as "like" an instrument in opening or closing "a way," revealing or concealing "an entrance or passageway;"
3. Specifically (a) a place so located as to give access to or control of a region;
4. A controlling or essential person or thing; and
5. A "keynote" person for a particular experience; authoritative position.

1 Peter 3:19–20 and 4:6 talks of Jesus's authority over hell as follows:

a) Preached unto spirits in hell (prison);

b) Which sometime were disobedient ... in the days of Noah, ... wherein few, that is (only), eight souls were saved by water.

Isaiah 5:14 describes hell as having the ability to be a *growing organism* to accommodate its occupants.

Jesus speaks of hell sixteen times in the New Testament. Two of these verses speak of the keys to hell. Matthew 16:18 describes hell as having doors or entry gates; "and the *gates (doors to hell's government)* of hell shall not prevail (not have power over) against it."

QUESTION: DID THE FATHER SHOW YOU HELL?

DEAN'S RESPONSE:

> To start, it's not unusual that Christians go to Heaven. That's what's supposed to happen to us. It's unusual for people (God's creatures) to go to hell. That is where we're not supposed to go.
>
> I didn't see hell. What happened was there were three times that Jesus said, "No. It's not your time, go back." And the first time He told me, "No. It's not your time, go back," my body wasn't ready experience wise. So, I went back and walked through Heaven. Then I got back to Jesus and He downloaded (thought-to-thought) some parables and things into me, and He said, "No. It's not your time, go back." And He took me to where, I would call, "the edge of Heaven." (Is there really an edge of Heaven? No. That's just the best way I can describe it.) But when I got

there, I could hear the screams and the hollers from hell. I could hear them. And I wanted to look over, but it wasn't His desire. It wasn't His desire that they be there, and it wasn't His desire that I look!

Now, what really got to me about hearing those sounds from hell is, I thought, I would hear sounds of, "Have mercy on us," "Get us out of here!" Instead, I heard cursing and (what I would call) tearing down God! That's what was coming from them. And I thought, "Well, that's outside of my box," because I figured, if you're going to be in hell, you're going be in hell, and you're going be asking God to forgive you.

But, again, in the Book of Revelation, there's a break during the tribulations and instead of the people turning to God, they curse Him. One Bible verse says: "He that is unjust, let him be unjust still: and he that is filthy, let him be filthy still: and he that is righteous, let him be righteous still: and he that is holy, let him be holy still." (Revelation 22:11)

So, even in hell, instead of turning to God, they can't, and they're cursing Him. And, again, "my box" was not that way. "My box" was being blown away, all of a sudden! I tell people all the time, "I'm not trying to keep people out of hell; I'm trying to get people in Heaven!"

Bill Wiese, he is the one who wrote the book, "23 Minutes in Hell." He and I did a meeting together. He did the "hell" part and I did the "Heaven" part. And I remember him coming up to me and shaking my hand and saying, "I wish I had gone to Heaven" and I just looked at him and smiled, because I was not going to say, "I wished I had gone to hell," you know? I'm not destined to hell. The sad thing about it is that he has to share "over and over" what it's like to go to hell, while I get to share what it was like to go to be with the Father and Jesus (in Heaven). You think about it! In sharing about Heaven, *I continue to experience it. Each time I experience it, it's a GREAT MOMENT!* Matter-of-fact, *IT'S BETTER EVERY MOMENT.* I tell people that the *MOMENT I WAS IN WAS GOOD, BUT THE NEXT MOMENT WAS EVEN BETTER!* It was like *THAT MOMENT I WAS REEXPERIENCING WAS SO MUCH BETTER THAN ANY THAT HAD EVER BEFORE EXISTED.* And Bill, sharing his experience over and over, guess what? He has to *continue to experience it!* He's experiencing *JUST THE OPPOSITE! HIS MOMENT IS A "TERRIBLE MOMENT," AND THE NEXT MOMENT IS EVEN "MORE TERRIBLE" THAN THAT MOMENT THAT NEVER EXISTED BEFORE!* You understand? We're, each, going the opposite way. And those people in hell are experiencing it "like" they have flesh! When you read about hell in the Bible, they're experiencing it "like" they have "flesh." You hear me? They're in their spiritual form, and yet they're experiencing it "like" they have flesh. Is that sad or is that sad?

QUESTION: SO, THEY CAN FEEL THE TORMENT?

DEAN'S RESPONSE:

YES.

QUESTION: WHAT CAUSED HIM TO HAVE THAT EXPERIENCE?

DEAN'S RESPONSE:

> He had an out-of-body experience or vision. I never read the book, but he told me that he woke up and he had "like" a vision "like" Peter had, when the sheets came down from Heaven; and he got to experience it that way. So, it wasn't a dream. It was "like" an open vision that just came to him.

Chapter 9

THE NECESSITY FOR PROPER WARFARE

DEAN'S QUESTION: WHY DO WE NEED PEOPLE TO PRAY FOR US?

DEAN'S RESPONSE:

> When we hear the spirit telling us to pray, our flesh becomes involved and says, "Aw, that's just me," "I don't know about that." See what I'm talking about? Instead of going by what the Spirit just said, we listen to our flesh.

AUDIENCE COMMENT:

> The Spirit will often give you like a picture of someone's face. I've had that experience; and when you see that person's face, you say, "Okay, what was that about?" And the flesh will say something like, "Oh, that was nothing!" The Spirit is supposed to say "pray," and we should immediately obey Him.

DEAN'S RESPONSE:

The Pastor talked about that earlier, in that sense about her son and grandson, and that she should have listened to the Spirit telling her to pray (and even continued to intercede, like my wife). The devil, he is not playing, you all, because he's taking people out!

One of the things of spiritual warfare that most people don't realize is (we know there are demons, devils, spirits, and all) that there are human beings on the planet that have been assigned to you. And they, literally, go through their chants with your name on it to hurt you. And most of us don't even battle against that part. My wife said something to me about when she was praying for me, she said, "Father, in the name of Jesus, I curse every negative word and every negative prayer that would be spoken over Dean. I thank you Lord that he will receive nothing but that which brings life." So, where would the negative prayers come from? Do you see what I mean? "Life and death are in the power of the tongue." Demonic tongue and human tongue, whether meaningfully or not meaningfully; purposefully or not purposefully.

And that realm knows just as much as this realm, that if we, on the planet, speak; they have permission to do things. So, in what we call spiritual warfare, you're not just battling demons, devils, etc. We're battling other human beings. This is something that we need to be aware of, that there are other human beings on the planet that are cursing you. And if you cause trouble in that demonic kingdom, you're going to have people assigned to you to curse you. Just like we have people assigned to us to pray for us.

If you want to know why some things are happening (over a period of time), it's because somebody is cursing you. So, you need to go after that person that's cursing you. You go after the spirit in that person, but you need to go after the person also.

Let's say, there's a witch, right now, that has your name. And you would say (in prayer), "Father, in the name of Jesus, I cancel the words and I bind up the words that that person has imparted (or is imparting) over me," and it has to stop! Not because the person wants to stop, but because of the word of God, they have to stop! And I pray that they come to receive salvation and know Jesus Christ as Lord and Saviour.

The other thing some people do is they send the words spoken against them back, praying that those words will fall on the person. I just don't do that. But there are people that have been assigned to Christians, who are working in the Kingdom of God, causing damage to Satan's kingdom. And sooner or later, you're going to come up on his radar and somebody is going to be assigned to you.

That's why most people doing what I do don't get a lot of people to pray for them. That's why the Bible tells us to pray for our pastors. And don't only pray for them when you think they're in trouble. You ought to pray for them all the time. I believe in what you call "prevention prayer." It doesn't have to happen! Do you understand? I've been in some places where Christians were not accepted. I accepted a New Age Conference. You get invited to speak in all kinds of places, and some people ask, "Aren't you afraid to speak in those kinds of places?" I don't want you to pray *"when we get into trouble!"* I want you to pray *"before we get into trouble!"*

When we went to New Zealand (the second time we went), they decided they would get about five hundred people to pray for us on a regular basis. It turned out to be fifty thousand. Then it ended up being over one hundred thousand. And they knew each person needing prayer by name. So, why wouldn't we have the results we had? And I say that because, if you're working in the Kingdom of God, you need people to pray for you. You don't need people to just say, "Oh, I'm going to pray for you." You need people who are really going to pray for you. One of my litmus tests is you get these little old ladies, they seem to really pray for people. If you find someone who is an intercessor and you know their name (whether they ever see you again or not), they are the ones you want praying for you. Those of us who do God's work, we usually don't have enough people praying for us. And usually I can tell that by the number of attacks that are coming upon that person.

PASTOR:

I realize now that that was my situation, because I have been causing havoc to the kingdom of darkness too much.

DEAN:

They don't want you there. They will go after everybody in your family!

PASTOR:

That's what they have done.

DEAN:

The devil doesn't go out to just mess with you; he goes out to do genocide. You caused great damage in his kingdom and he's going to make sure the next of your generation doesn't. So, you need more people to pray for you. You'll need people who are going to constantly pray for you, even if they're never going to see you again. A lot of people "say" they're going to pray for me, but it's just a by-word or the expected thing to say.

When I was up in Heaven, this is what Jesus said to me, "If my people, who are called by my name, would humble themselves and pray, and seek my face, and turn from their wicked ways and pray, I will heal their land." He didn't say, "I'll give them a new president." He didn't say, "I'll bring all the Senate in and they'd be believers." He said, "I'll heal their land." And we in America probably have more information on prayer than most nations. But when I was with the Father and Jesus, you could see where Jesus was sending angels. They're only going to be sent where prayer is being made, and on a scale of one-to-ten, I saw more angels going to about a nine to China. And in our area, about a four. We have a lot of information on it, but we don't pray. You that are in ministry know what I'm saying is true.

Because, if you call a thirty-day prayer time here, you may start off with a good crowd, but by the time the thirtieth day comes, you may be here by yourself (or one or two others). Yet we want to see results. And faithfulness. So, if you "say" you're going to do it, even when you don't "feel" like it; in fact, that's the time (and you've heard it before), that "you really" should do it.

PASTOR:

I know that's one of the weaknesses in our church (and it really grieves me) is faithfulness. People make promises, and pledges, and all of that, but they're not faithful. And a pastor needs faithfulness, people they can depend on to do whatever they promised or committed themselves to do. They need to realize that they're not being faithful to you, but they're being faithful to Jesus. That's the problem, Dean. Actually, they did make the promise to me, and therefore, there is no resolve to keep it. Because in their minds, they were only speaking to me and not to God. They think they're impressing the flesh or stroking the flesh, but it, ultimately, results in a disappointment.

Bibliography

1. Heaven Is For Real; Todd Burpo (with Lynn Vincent) 2010; Thomas Nelson Publishers, Nashville, TN. 37214.

2. Heaven Changes Everything; Todd & Sonja Burpo, 2012, 2014; W Publishing Group, an Imprint of Thomas Nelson, Nashville, TN. 37214

3. Heaven is Beautiful; Peter Baldwin Panagore, 2015; Hampton Roads Publishing Company, Inc., Charlottesville, VA. 22906.

4. Heaven is Real (But So is Hell); Vassula Ryden/The Foundation for True Life in God, 2013, Geneva, Switzerland; Published by Alexian, an imprint of Alexian Limited, New York*Bath.

5. Heaven is Beyond Your Wildest Expectations; Sid Roth & Lonnie Lane, 2012; Messianic Vision; Destiny Image Publishers, Inc., Shippensburg, PA. 17257.

6. In Heaven (Experiencing The Throne of God); Dean Braxton 2015; AEONS, Inc.

7. The Map of Heaven; Eben Alexander, M.D. (with Ptolemy Tompkins), 2014; Simon & Schuster Paperbacks, A Division of Simon & Schuster, Inc., New York, NY. 10020.

8. To Heaven and Back; Mary C. Neal, M.D., 2011; Waterbrook Press, Colorado Springs, CO. 80921.

9. The Boy Who Came Back From Heaven; Kevin & Alex Malarkey, 2010, 2011; Tyndale Momentum, an Imprint of Tyndale House Publishers, Inc., Carol Stream, IL. 60188.

10. 90 Minutes In Heaven, Don Piper (with Cecil Murphey), 2004; Published by Revell, a division of Baker Publishing Group, Grand Rapids, MI. 49516.

11. When Will The Heaven Begin? Ally Breedlove (with Ken Abraham), 2013; Penguin Group, New York, NY. 10014.

12. Appointments with Heaven, Dr. Reggie Anderson (with Jennifer Schuchmann) 2013; Tyndale Momentum, an Imprint of Tyndale House Publishers, Inc., Carol Stream, IL. 60188.

13. Chasing Heaven, Crystal McVea and Tresniowski, 2016; Howard Books an Imprint of Simon & Schuster, Inc., New York, NY. 10020.

14. Glimpsing Heaven, Judy Bachrach, 2014; National Geographic Society; Washington, D.C., 20036.

15. Opening Heaven's Door, Patricia Pearson, Atria Paperback an Imprint of Simon & Schuster, Inc., New York, NY. 10020.

16. Touching Heaven, Dr. Chauncey Crandall (with Kris Bearss), 2015; Faith Words Hachette Book Group; New York, NY. 10104.

17. A Divine Revelation of Heaven, Mary K Baxter (with Dr. T.L. Lowery), 1998; Whitaker House; New Kensington, PA. 15068.

18. Miracles From Heaven, Christy Wilson Beam, 2015; Hachette Book Group; New York, NY. 10104

19. More Glimpses of Heaven, Trudy Harris, RN, 2010; Published by Revell; Grand Rapids, MI. 49516.

20. Falling Into Heaven, Mickey Robinson, 2014; BroadStreet Publishing Group, LLC; Racine, Washington, USA.

21. Flight to Heaven, Captain Dale Black (with Ken Gire), 2010; Published by Bethany House Publishers; Bloomington, MN. 55438.

22. My Journey to Heaven, Marvin J. Besteman (with Lorilee Cracker), 2012; Published by Revell; Grand Rapids, MI. 49516.

23. Waking Up In Heaven, Crystal McVea and Alex Tresniowski, 2013; Howard Books a Division of Simon & Schuster, Inc., New York, NY. 10020.

24. Proof of Heaven, Eben Alexander, M.D., 2012; Simon & Schuster Paperbacks a Division of Simon & Schuster, Inc.; New York, NY. 10020.

25. Deep Worship In Heaven, Dean Braxton, 2017; Braxton Press Productions; Printed in the United States of America.

26. My Time In Heaven, Richard Sigmund, 2004, 2010; Whitaker House; New Kensington, PA. 15068.

27. Visits from Heaven, Pete Deison, 2016; W Publishing Group an Imprint of Thomas Nelson; Nashville, TN. 37214.

28. Within Heaven's Gates, Rebecca Springer, 1984, 2012; Whitaker House; New Kensington, PA. 15068.

29. The Day I Died, Freddy Vest, 2014; Published by Charisma House; Lake Mary, FL. 32746.

30. What Happens When I Die? Bill Wiese, 2013; Published by Charisma House; Lake Mary, FL. 32746.

31. When Breath Becomes Air, Paul Kalanithi, 2016; Published by Random House; USA.

32. Angels in the ER, Robert D. Lesslie, M.D., 2008; Published by MJF Books Fine Communications; New York, NY. 10001.

33. A Message of Hope from the Angels, Lorna Byrne, 2012; Atria Books a Division of Simon & Schuster, Inc.; New York, NY. 10020.

34. Into the Light, John Lerma, M.D., 2007; New Page Books a Division of The Career Press, Inc.; Pompton Plains, NJ. 07444.

35. God and the Afterlife, Jeffrey Long, M.D. (with Paul Perry), 2016; Harper One an Imprint of Harper Collins Publishers; New York, NY. 10007.

36. When God Doesn't Make Sense, Dr. James Dobson, 1993; Tyndale House Publishers; Carol Stream, IL. 60188.

37. Ghost Boy, Martin Pistorius (with Megan Lloyd Davies), 2013; Nelson Books an Imprint of Thomas Nelson; Nashville, TN. 37214.

38. Self-Centeredness: The Source of All Grief, Andrew Wommack, 2012; Published by Andrew Wommack Ministries, Inc.; Colorado Springs, CO. 80907.

39. 23 Minutes In Hell, Bill Wiese, 2006; Published by Charisma House; Lake Mary, FL. 32746.

40. A Divine Revelation of Hell, Mary K. Baxter, 1993; Whitaker House; Springdale, PA. 15144.

41. Not Yet, Jeff O'Driscoll. M.D., 2017; Jeff's Publishing Company; Middletown, DE.,

42. Dying to Wake Up, Dr. Rajiv Parti (with Paul Perry), 2016; Atria Books, an Imprint of Simon & Schuster, Inc., New York, NY. 10020

About the Author

Donzella Ervin is a retired Senior Pastor of the Kingdom of God Tabernacle Church. She and her deceased husband, Richard Ervin, founded the church in 2004.

In 2005, she authored the book entitled, "What is Deliverance? & Some of the Ways the Holy Spirit Demonstrates It." This book was birthed out of the deliverance experiences the Holy Spirit manifested during her pastoral ministry; five hundred copies were sold.

She authored four other books, which were published in 2014, but due to the recurred illness of her husband and other family tragedies, she was unable to devote her attention to having them printed. Now she believes that this is her season to release them. The titles are: "Disconnect to Reconnect," "The Sixth and Seventh Day," "The True Vine," and "What is Salvation? And How Is It Defined in the Scriptures?"